YOUNG STUDENTS

Learning Library

VOLUME 5

Cell–Computer

WEEKLY READER BOOKS
MIDDLETOWN·CONNECTICUT

PHOTO CREDITS

BBC HULTON PICTURE LIBRARY page 525(bottom right); 566(top left); 611(center right). THE BETTMANN ARCHIVE page 531(both pics); 532(top left); 566(bottom right); 589(top right); 591(bottom right). BIOPHOTO page 590(bottom left). BRITISH FILM INSTITUTE page 511(top right). BRITISH MUSEUM page 572(bottom left); 611(top right). BUREAU OF INDIAN AFFAIRS page 543(top right). CBS Records page 545(top right). J. ALLAN CASH page 557(bottom right); 615(bottom right). THE CHRISTIAN SCIENCE PUBLISHING SOCIETY page 547(bottom right). CHUBB page 624(top left). CIRCUS WORLD MUSEUM, BARABOO, WIS. page 552. CLAYTON page 511(bottom right). COLONIAL WILLIAMSBURG page 596(bottom left). COURTAULDS LTD page 521(top right). ARMANDO CURCIO EDITORE, SPA page 505(center right); 508(bottom left); 510(both pics); 513(top right); 514(both pics); 517(bottom right); 535(top right); 541(top right); 543(bottom right); 544(bottom left); 548(top left); 549(top right); 555(bottom right); 568(top left & bottom center); 570(bottom left); 571(bottom right); 573(bottom right); 579(center right); 584(top left); 589(bottom right); 592(4 coins); 602(top left). DEPT OF TRADE & INDUSTRY page 623(bottom). EDITORIAL PHOTOCOLOR ARCHIVES page 578(top left). MARY EVANS PICTURE LIBRARY page 513(bottom right); 566 (bottom left); 611(bottom right). FERRANTI page 621(top right). FOTOMAS page 619(center top). GLASGOW DENTAL HOSPITAL page 527(bottom left). HENRY GRANT page 580(top left). SONIA HALLIDAY page 545(bottom right); 546(top left). ROBERT HARDING ASSOCIATES page 593(top right). MICHAEL HOLFORD page 512(top left). RICHARD HOOVER page 600(top right). HULTON page 619(bottom right). IBM page 621(bottom right). IMITOR page 585(right)/Peter Green. INSTITUTO FOTOGRAFICO, FLORENCE page 513(bottom). ERNEST PAUL LEHMANN page 594(top left). LIBRARY OF CONGRESS page 569(bottom). WILLIAM MACQUITTY page 540(top left). MANSELL COLLECTION page 515(bottom); 530(top left); 532(bottom left); 539(top left, top right); 548(bottom left); 561(bottom right); 585(center bottom); 605(top right); 620(top left). PAT MORRIS page 570(bottom center). MOZARTEUM SALZBURG page 619(bottom left). NASA page 597(bottom right). NHPA page 503(top right); 559(center right); 590(top right). NATIONAL ARCHIVES page 567(bottom left). NATIONAL COAL BOARD page 586(top center). NATIONAL GALLERY OF ART, WASHINGTON DC page 509(top). NATIONAL PORTRAIT GALLERY page 513(top right). PETER NEWARK/WESTERN AMERICANA page 522(bottom right). NO-VOSTI page 614(bottom). POPPERFOTO page 562(bottom left); 563(top left). THE POST OFFICE page 614(top left). REX FEATURES LTD page 514(top left). SACU page 538(top right); 540(bottom left). SCALA page 503(bottom right); 512(bottom right); 547(top right). G. SCHIRMER, INC. page 544(top left). CHARLES SCRIBNER'S SONS page 533(top). SEAPHOT page 571(top left). SMITHSONIAN INSTITUTION page 606(top left). SONY UK page 612(bottom left). SPECTRUM COLOUR LIBRARY page 523(top right); 548(top left). SPINK page 592(top right). SWISS NATIONAL TOURIST OFFICE page 517(top left). UPI page 574(top). ZEFA page 500, 519(top right); 527(top & center right); 536(top left); 537(bottom right); 538(center left); 540(top left); 554(bottom left); 556(top right); 557(bottom right); 558(top left); 561(top right); 577(top right); 581(top right); 587(top right); 597(top right); 598(bottom left); 601(bottom right); 615(top right).

Copyright © 1990, 1989, 1988, 1982, 1977 Field Publications; 1974, 1972 by Funk & Wagnalls, Inc., & Field Publications.

ISBN 0-8374-6035-2

CONTENTS

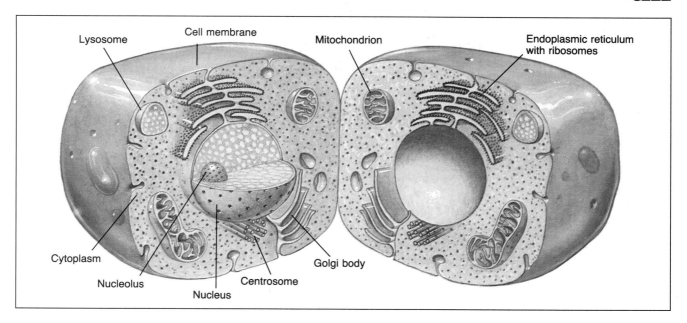

Lysosome Cell membrane Mitochondrion Endoplasmic reticulum with ribosomes

Cytoplasm Nucleolus Nucleus Centrosome Golgi body

CELL About 300 years ago, Anton van Leeuwenhoek built a *microscope* and became one of the first people to look at the tiny, usually unseen, world that surrounds us all. The idea of the microscope had been discovered by Zacharias Janssen in 1590, but Leeuwenhoek was one of the first to use it to observe and then to write down what he saw. A microscope is like a powerful magnifying glass. It lets us observe things that are too small for our eyes to see.

Leeuwenhoek wondered what a drop of water would look like through his microscope. He was amazed to find that there were many tiny living things squirming about in the water. It was the first time anyone had seen single-celled animals.

Robert Hooke, an English scientist, developed an even more powerful microscope. He placed a slice of cork under his microscope and studied it. What he saw reminded him of many small rooms arranged side by side. Small rooms are sometimes called cells, so Hooke named the tiny bits of cork "cells." He later saw that living cells (cork is dead) are not vacant rooms but are filled with a juicy material.

Scientists were not sure exactly what cells were for a long time. But gradually several scientists put forth ideas. One gave the juicy material a name—*protoplasm*. Another identified a specific body within the cell as the *nucleus*. Scientists became certain that plant cells were basic parts of the living plant. But animal cells do not have the clear outline of plant cells. A German botanist, Mathias Schleiden, and a zoologist, Theodor Schwann, announced in 1838 that cells are the basic "building blocks" of all living things, or *organisms*.

Some simple organisms are only one cell. Bacteria and protozoa are one-celled organisms. Other organisms are much more complex. A human body may be made of about one trillion (a million million) cells.

Cell Structure and Work You have just read that every living thing is made of cells, and that cells are made of something called protoplasm. Does this mean that all plants and animals are made of the same material? How can such different organisms as cows, ants, flowers, and human beings be made of the same colorless, jellylike substance? The answer is that each kind of plant and animal has its own special kind of protoplasm. A cow's special protoplasm makes that animal

▲ *If an animal cell were sliced in half it would look something like this. In the center is the nucleus. Surrounding it are various structures, each of which plays a part in the cell "factory." The endoplasmic reticulum is where proteins are made. The lysosomes act as the cell's scavengers. They break down bacteria. Golgi bodies appear to store chemicals and proteins produced in the ribosomes. Mitochondria are the cell's power stations. They contain enzymes that trigger the conversion of food into energy.*

Not all cells are so tiny that you cannot see them. The yolk of an ostrich egg is actually a single cell. It is about the size of an orange.

◄ *The thrill of the circus reaches everyone, young and old. Here, acrobats from the Moscow State Circus of the Soviet Union perform in the ring.* (See CIRCUS.)

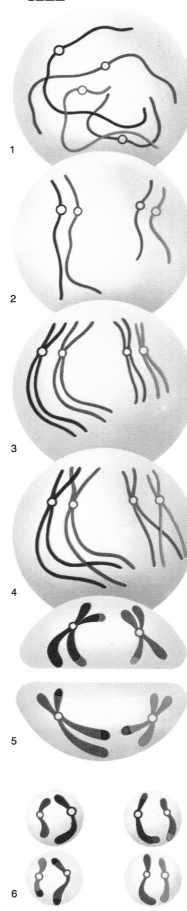

a cow, not an ant, flower, or human being.

Every cell has two main parts—the cytoplasm and the nucleus. The nucleus is usually a ball-shaped structure near the center of the cell. The protoplasm outside the nucleus is the *cytoplasm.* An outer envelope called the *cell membrane* holds the cell juices together.

A cell is a living thing. It performs certain activities, or *functions*, to stay alive. For example, a cell takes in food and oxygen, and gets rid of its waste materials. Food, oxygen, and waste materials pass in and out of the cell through the cell membrane. The nucleus is the most important part of the cell. It regulates all of the cell's functions. The cytoplasm contains several tiny structures called *organelles,* which carry out cell functions.

A plant cell has parts that an animal cell does not. The plant cell has a *cell wall* surrounding the cell membrane. This cell wall contains *cellulose,* a hard substance. Cellulose helps to make the cell stiff. The stiffness enables plants to resist wind and to stand without bones. Plant cells also have *chloroplasts* containing *chlorophyll,* a substance that helps plants make food.

Special Cells   Not all cells, even in a single plant or animal, are alike. Some of them have taken on special tasks, and their structure and function permit them to fulfill these tasks. In the human body, muscles, nerves, skin,

◀ Meiosis *is a special kind of cell division that takes place when egg or sperm cells are being produced. The number of chromosomes in a cell is halved in its granddaughter cells. (1) The chromosomes are first long and threadlike. (2) They pair up and shorten. (3) Each chromosome duplicates. (4) The paired chromosomes exchange parts. (5) The cell divides. Each daughter cell has four chromosomes. (6) These cells divide. Each of the four granddaughter cells inherits two chromosomes.*

blood, and bones are all composed of special types of cells. Red blood cells, for example, are adapted to absorb great amounts of oxygen from the lungs and then to "trade" it with various other cells for carbon dioxide. Muscle cells are adapted to contract or expand. Some do it in response to voluntary instructions from the brain, such as to move an arm or leg. Other muscle cells, such as those in the heart, work without voluntary instructions. Highly specialized nerve cells carry the instructions to the muscles, in addition to carrying out other tasks.

Reproduction   Like all other living things, cells reproduce. The nucleus performs most of the work of making new cells. A cell forms two new cells when its nucleus and then its cytoplasm split in half. The splitting is called *mitosis.* Exactly what "tells" a cell to split is not yet known. Scientists think the cell gathers enough material for building and energy. The "grown-up" cell then seems to be ready for mitosis. The way meiosis occurs is shown in the diagram.

Stringy-looking objects called *chromosomes* are found in the nucleus. They contain thousands of smaller structures called *genes.* Genes are the messengers of life. Each gene carries certain "special instructions." For example, pairs of genes carry the orders that make a baby's eyes brown. All the genes together dictate what a living thing is to be.

Special cells are involved in reproduction of living things. The nuclei of egg cells from females and sperm cells from males split in a special way called *meiosis.* For example, each regular human cell contains 46 single chromosomes or 23 pairs. If the one male cell and one female cell that join to make a new organism each contained 46 chromosomes, the united cell would have 92 chromosomes. This would prevent reproduction of a new human being. Each male and

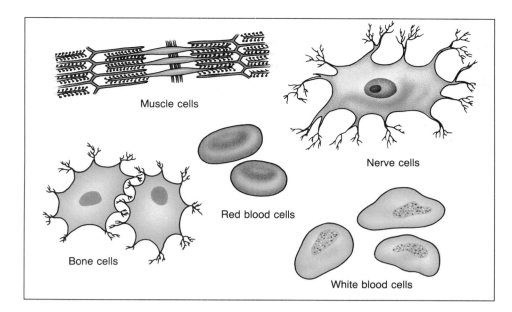

Muscle cells

Nerve cells

Red blood cells

Bone cells

White blood cells

▲ *This microscopic organism is called a* Paramecium. *It is made up of just one cell and looks like a tiny speck to the naked eye.* (Above left) *Different types of human cells.*

female cell, however, undergoes a special kind of splitting, in which 46 chromosomes are reduced to 23. Meiosis and the way genes work is the subject of the science of *genetics*.

ALSO READ: ANIMAL, BLOOD, BONE, EGG, GENETICS, MICROSCOPE, MUSCLE, NERVOUS SYSTEM, PLANT, REPRODUCTION, SKIN.

CELLINI, BENVENUTO (1500– 1571) "Benvenuto!"—Welcome!— cried the father of Benvenuto Cellini, when his first son was born nearly 20 years after his daughter. This very welcome baby boy grew up in the art center of Florence, Italy, and became a famous goldsmith and sculptor. He studied for a time with the great sculptor Michelangelo. But Cellini had a short temper and quarreled often with people, so he frequently moved to new places to work.

Cellini's work was much in demand, but only a few pieces survive today. One small piece is a saltcellar of gold he made for King Francis I of France in 1543. Two years later he made the large sculpture shown here of Perseus holding up the head of Medusa, whom he had just beheaded. This statue stood dramatically in the Loggia dei Lanzi, a portico in Flor-

ence. It is thought to be one of the finest Renaissance sculptures.

One other great work of Cellini still lives—his autobiography. A worker in the sculptor's studio took down Cellini's words as he dictated the story of his life. It is still widely read today and gives a fascinating view of life in an exciting time. Strangely enough, Cellini's autobiography may be his greatest work.

ALSO READ: ART HISTORY, MICHELANGELO BUONARROTI.

CENSORSHIP If an author writes a book containing criticism of the government, and the government then prevents the book from being published, that author's work has been *censored*. In a free country such as the United States, people are mostly able to read and watch whatever they want. Only things that offend the majority, such as obscenity, are censored. But in many other countries, especially those in the Communist world, there is *state censorship*. The government censors newspapers, books, films, plays and television. The state censor has the power to ban anything that is felt to be critical of the government or the ruling party.

In the free world, it is up to the

▲ Perseus *by Benvenuto Cellini.*

There were creatures living on Earth about 350 million years ago that were very similar to today's centipedes.

The longest known centipede is a 46-legged giant that lives in the forests of South America. It is about 10 inches (25 cm) long and 1 inch (2.5 cm) wide.

individual to choose what to read or to watch on TV. Some industries, such as the motion picture industry, have "guidelines" to help filmmakers decide what should, or should not, be shown. The Motion Picture Association of American gives a seal of approval to films it thinks suitable for the general public. This kind of judgment is called *self-censorship*.

In wartime, letters from soldiers overseas may be read by a censor to make sure they do not contain information of use to the enemy. But in the United States in peacetime, "freedom of information" is generally believed to be the best guarantee of liberty.

CENSUS see POPULATION.

CENTAUR see ANIMALS OF MYTH AND LEGEND.

CENTIPEDES AND MILLIPEDES The many-legged small animals known as centipedes and millipedes are found in most parts of the world. Common house centipedes usually live in damp places such as basements. Millipedes creep through soil or rotting wood.

Centipedes and millipedes look something like worms with many legs. Their bodies are divided into many sections called *segments*, ar-

ranged one behind another. Centipedes have one pair of legs on each segment. Millipedes have two pairs on each segment.

Centipedes are swift-moving animals that eat insects and sometimes plants. They kill their prey with poisonous claws. The name "centipede" means "hundred-footed," but some centipedes have fewer and some have more legs. Common house centipedes have only 30 legs. They eat harmful insects such as mosquitoes. They may sting if handled roughly, but the sting of a house centipede is not serious. There are 1,500 kinds of centipedes in the world, some with as many as 346 legs. Large centipedes in the tropics are poisonous enough to be dangerous to humans.

The name "millipede" means "thousand-footed," but no millipede really has that many legs. Millipedes live in damp, dark places such as rotting logs, where they can find decaying plant matter, their favorite food. They move very slowly in spite of their many legs. You can pick up a millipede and watch waves of motion pass through its body and legs. Millipedes cannot bite, and they usually coil up when disturbed.

Centipedes and millipedes belong to two different classes in the big animal kingdom group called *arthropods*. All arthropods are *invertebrates* (animals without backbones) with jointed legs and segmented bodies. Insects, spiders, and crustaceans are also arthropods.

ALSO READ: ANIMAL KINGDOM, CRUSTACEAN, INSECT, SPIDER.

▼ Centipedes and millipedes are both arthropods. But while centipedes are flesh-eaters, millipedes live on plant material.

Millipede

Centipede

CENTRAL AFRICAN REPUBLIC The Central African Republic is one of Africa's youngest nations. It is located in the center of the continent. The countries surrounding it are Chad, Sudan, Cameroon, the Congo, and Zaire. The largest city is

CENTRAL AFRICAN REPUBLIC

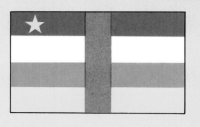

Capital City: Bangui (474,000 people).

Area: 240,553 square miles (622,984 sq. km).

Population: 3,000,000.

Government: Republic, ruled by a Military Committee.

Natural Resources: Diamonds, lumber.

Export Products: Lumber, coffee, diamonds, cotton.

Unit of Money: Franc of the African Financial Community.

Official Language: French.

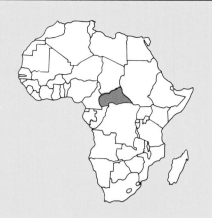

Bangui, the capital. (See the map with the article on AFRICA.)

The Central African Republic has a warm climate. Rain falls nearly every day during the rainy season. At other times the country is hot and dry. The Central African Republic is a beautiful country. The southern part is covered by tropical rain forests. Monkeys, gorillas, chimpanzees, hippopotamuses, snakes, crocodiles, and colorful birds live there. To the north is a rolling, grassy plain, or *savanna*. Among the many savanna animals are antelopes, hyenas, and lions. Many tourists visit the country to hunt, or just to take photographs in the savanna.

The Central African Republic is the size of California and Idaho together. But it has very few people for its size. They speak many different languages because they belong to different tribes. When people from different tribes want to talk to each other, they speak in French or in Sangho, a language known by most of the people.

Most of the people are poor. They live in thatched huts in tiny villages. Some of them raise cattle. Others are farmers who grow cotton, coffee, and grain. The country also produces some rubber, palm oil, and diamonds. It has no outlet to the sea, no railroad, and few roads, so it is very hard for the people to sell their products, or to buy things they need, such

as modern tools. Many older people cannot read or write, but many children are now receiving an elementary school education.

For several centuries, the area was subjected to slave raids by Muslim Arabs and others. In 1894 the French organized the area as Ubangi-Shari, which later became part of the French Equatorial Africa. The people of Ubangi-Shari rebelled and, in 1960, established the independent Central African Republic. Jean-Bédel Bokassa seized control of the country in 1966. He declared himself Emperor Bokassa I of the Central African Empire in 1976. In 1979 he was ousted and the Central African Republic was reestablished.

ALSO READ: AFRICA.

▲ *A child in the Central African Republic beats the drum in his village.*

CENTRAL AMERICA Central America is an *isthmus*, or land bridge, connecting North and South America. This long, narrow neck of land was forced out of the sea by volcanic action millions of years ago. Even now, active and extinct volcanoes stick up in the mountain ranges that run along the western side of the isthmus. Seven countries lie along this strip from north to south—Guatemala, Belize, El Salvador, Honduras, Nicaragua, Costa Rica, and Panama. The republic of Panama occupies the isthmus that connects

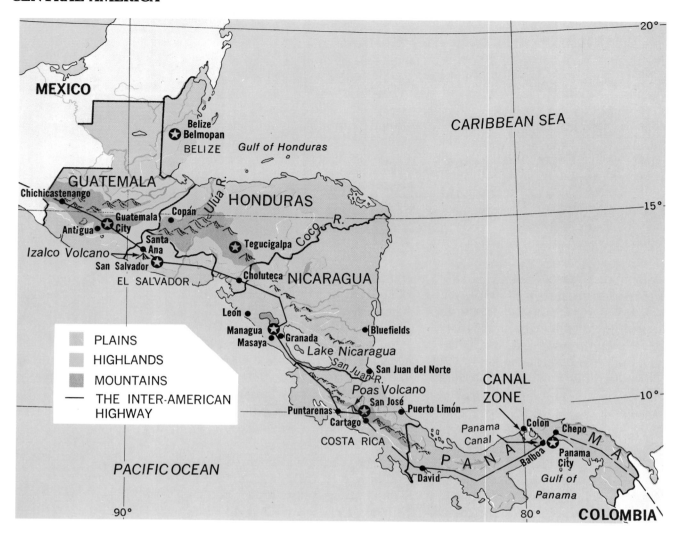

PLAINS

HIGHLANDS

MOUNTAINS

THE INTER-AMERICAN HIGHWAY

Central and South America. Panamanians do not consider themselves Central Americans. Some people mistakenly think Mexico is part of Central America, but it is really part of North America.

Coastal areas on the east are flat, swampy, and thick with green jungle. Temperatures are hot at sea level throughout the region. Most of the capitals and other cities are built in the highlands, which are cool even near the equator.

Nearly all the people are Indian, Spanish, or a mixture of the two. Along the Caribbean coast of some countries are populations of blacks. Most of the people work small, poor farms. Their lives have been changing, however, since the completion of the Inter-American Highway from the Texas border to the Panama Canal in the 1960's. The road was paid for chiefly by the United States. The countries themselves are building feeder roads to the big highway, and farmers now use the all-weather road to move their crops to market. The Central American Common Market, an economic union including Guatemala, El Salvador, Honduras, Nicaragua, and Costa Rica, uses the road for the exchange of goods among the countries. The wealth of Central America comes mostly from farms. Bananas, coffee, sugarcane, cotton, and corn are the chief crops.

Long before Christ, the Maya Indians developed the first great civilization in the Americas, in what is now Belize and Guatemala. Columbus first explored the Caribbean coast in 1502, and Spanish forces conquered Central America in 1525. Spain ruled the area for 300 years, until the 1820's, when it lost control of most of its New World colonies. But Spanish influence had been implanted in the culture.

All Central America, except Panama, was ruled briefly by a Mexican empire under Augustín de Iturbide. After the downfall of Iturbide, a Central American confederation was established. But political fights and nationalism led to the dissolution of this confederation in 1839. One by one, the states of Guatemala, El Salvador, Honduras, Nicaragua, and Costa Rica became independent republics. Panama was part of the South American nation of Colombia until it broke away in 1903. At the time, the United States was negotiating to build the Panama Canal. The Panamanians wanted the canal built, but Colombia was withholding permission. The Panamanians declared independence and gave the U.S. permission to build the canal. For more than a century, these republics fought among themselves over land, borders, and canal-building rights. Several attempts to form Central American unions failed. U.S. policies were not always wel-comed. Today, the Organization of Central American States and the Central American Common Market are helping to unite the republics and solve problems.

Spanish is the main language in Central America, though many Indians still speak their old tribal languages and dialects. Most people in Central America live in the valleys and beside the mountains that run along the Pacific coast. Severe earthquakes sometimes hit this area. The densely populated city of Managua in Nicaragua was struck by an earthquake in 1972. It leveled 70 percent of the city and left more than 10,000 dead.

The population of all the Central American countries is increasing rapidly. Panama attracted many immigrants from Jamaica and other islands in the West Indies, as well as from its neighbor, Colombia. But natural increase accounts for approximately three percent annual growth in population. Today the seven Central American countries have about 29 million people.

ALSO READ: CONQUISTADOR; INDIANS, AMERICAN; *each country mentioned.*

Of all the Central American countries, Nicaragua has the smallest number of people to the square mile, only 63 (24 per square km). But this country has also had the largest population increase over the past few years.

◄ *Guatemalans on the steps of the church in Chichicastenango, one of the country's market towns. About half of Guatemala's people are Indians; the remainder are Ladinos—of mixed Spanish and Indian ancestry.*

CENTRAL INTELLIGENCE AGENCY In relations between nations, some matters are dealt with in secret. Gathering *intelligence*, or secret information, is the task of the Central Intelligence Agency (CIA). The CIA is the chief intelligence-gathering organization of the U.S. Government.

The CIA was set up in 1947 to bring together the espionage (the practice of spying) and counter-espionage activities of several government departments. It works directly under the National Security Council. Its director and deputy director are appointed by the President, subject to the advice and consent of the Senate.

The CIA is active at home and overseas. For example, rebels trained by the CIA have opposed the anti-American governments in Cuba and Nicaragua.

ALSO READ: SPY

CENTRIFUGAL FORCE see ORBIT.

CERAMICS see POTTERY AND CHINA.

CEREALS see GRAIN, RICE.

CERVANTES, MIGUEL DE (1547–1616) "Dear reader, pardon my poor child's faults," Cervantes wrote in a preface to his book, *Don Quixote*. He need not have apologized for his literary "child." It is a masterpiece of world literature.

Cervantes was born in Alcala de Henares, Spain. His full name was Miguel de Cervantes Saavedra. He joined the army in 1570 and was wounded in a battle against the Turks. He left the army in 1575 to go back to Spain. Barbary pirates captured his ship, and he was sold as a slave. He tried to escape many times but did not get his freedom for five years. At that time, his family was able to pay his ransom.

Cervantes returned to Spain and wrote many poems, plays, and stories. None of them were very successful. He became a tax collector, but he failed in the job. He was twice imprisoned for not paying debts. The idea of *Don Quixote* came to him while he was in jail. It is the amusing story of a charming but awkward, aging, scrawny gentleman who thinks he is a knight in armor. He worries his family by leaving home to do battle against evil. His horse is a bony creature named Rosinante, and his servant is the fat and jolly Sancho Panza. Windmills are giants to Don Quixote, and he attacks them with his lance. This book makes fun of knighthood and the manner of his day. A modern musical play based on the story is called *Man of La Mancha*.

ALSO READ: KNIGHTHOOD, NOVEL, SPANISH HISTORY.

CEYLON see SRI LANKA.

CÉZANNE, PAUL (1839–1906) Paul Cézanne was a French painter who changed the style of painting popular in his time. His work led away from the realistic paintings of people and places toward the abstract art that followed in the 1900's. Cézanne enjoyed the shapes and composition of his subjects. Many people say he was the greatest artist of the past hundred years.

Cézanne lived in Aix-en-Provence. He was the son of a banker who did not want his son to be an artist. Paul finally got his father's permission to study paintings in Paris. He did not paint well at first. He became friendly with artists called *Impressionists*. He tried but never quite achieved their way of painting.

Cervantes' great masterpiece has brought the word "quixotic," meaning impractical, into our language. And when people use the phrase "tilting at windmills," they mean fighting against imaginary difficulties.

▲ *Cervantes, Spanish author of* Don Quixote.

He went back home in 1886. He became known as the leader of the *Post-Impressionists* (the painters *after* the Impressionists). He did his most important paintings in Aix, including those of Mont Saint-Victoire.

Look at Cézanne's *Still Life With Apples and Peaches* shown here. Do you get the feeling that the objects seem to be falling off the table? The pitcher is almost floating in midair. You may wonder why. It is because Cézanne had a new, unusual idea about perspective. Cézanne often painted that way, seeming to ignore the laws of gravity. See how clear his colors are. Cézanne used perspective and color differently from earlier artists. His ideas soon led to a new and different kind of painting that came to be called *cubism*.

ALSO READ: ART HISTORY, IMPRESSIONISM, MODERN ART, PAINTING.

CHAD The Republic of Chad, the fifth largest country in Africa, is eight times the size of Illinois. Chad is in the center of northern Africa. It is completely surrounded by other countries. (See the map with the article on AFRICA.)

Chad is named for Lake Chad, which lies on the western border of the country. The lake may be as large as 10,000 square miles (25,900 sq. km) during the wet season. It shrinks to about 4,000 square miles (10,360

sq. km) during the dry season.

The northern region of Chad is part of the Sahara Desert, scorching hot by day and freezing cold at night. The center portion of the country is a dry land of treeless plains. The southern area gets plenty of rain and is richly covered with grass and trees.

Natives of Chad are called Chadians. The people of the northern and central areas are mostly nomads who live in tents and move to find grazing for their herds. The people in the south live on small farms and raise cotton, peanuts, and livestock. Most of Chad's nomads follow the Muslim religion, but many of the southern people follow native African religions, and a few are Christians.

Very little of the early history of Chad is known, although it is believed

▲ Still Life With Apples and Peaches *by Paul Cézanne. National Gallery of Art, Washington, D.C. Gift of Eugene and Agnes Meyer.*

During his life, Paul Cézanne sold no paintings and won no prizes for his work. A year after his death a large exhibition of his paintings was held in Paris. This exhibition had a great influence on many famous artists, including Georges Braque, Henri Matisse, and Pablo Picasso.

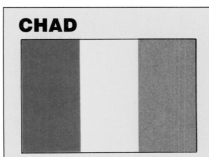

CHAD

Capital City: N'Djamena (510,000 people).
Area: 495,791 square miles (1,284,000 sq. km).
Population: 5,700,000.
Government: Republic.
Natural Resources: Bauxite, gold, uranium (all undeveloped).
Export Products: Cotton, meat and cattle, fish.
Unit of Money: Franc of the African Financial Community.
Official Language: French.

▲ *Two young girls in the colorful dress of Chad in north-central Africa.*

▲ *Samuel de Champlain, founder of the settlement at Quebec, Canada.*

How many ways are there of arranging 6 books on a shelf? This is a question connected with an area of probability called *permutation*. You can arrange 6 books on a shelf in 720 different ways—1 × 2 × 3 × 4 × 5 × 6 = 720.

that kingdoms once flourished there. The French invaded Chad and defeated the local chieftains in 1897. Chad became a French colony in French Equatorial Africa in 1913 and gained independence in 1960.

During the 1970's, the country suffered severely from a sub-Sahara drought. Farmland became sandy desert. Thousands of persons died. The country was also wracked by political fighting. In 1975, military forces overthrew the government. In 1983, France sent troops to oppose Libyan-backed rebels. By 1987, Libyan and French troops had left Chad.

ALSO READ: AFRICA.

CHAMPLAIN, SAMUEL DE (about 1567–1635) Samuel de Champlain was the founder of Quebec. He was born in France and traveled as a young man. The French king, Henry IV, liked Champlain's stories of his journeys so much that he named him Royal Geographer. Champlain was sent to Canada. He liked it and decided to establish French settlements there. He succeeded in founding a colony at Quebec in 1608, and he dedicated the rest of his life to the colony.

He discovered Lake Champlain, on the border of New York State. It is a long, narrow water body straddling the U.S.–Canadian border, and is the fourth largest freshwater lake in the U.S. Champlain later led a band of Huron Indians in a rash attack against an Iroquois village. He was badly wounded and barely escaped. Too sick to travel, he spent the winter hiding in a Huron village. The next July he was able to return to Quebec, where he was hailed as a man returned from the dead.

Champlain has been called the "father of New France," and he deserves the title. Before the end of his life, he saw his colony firmly established. Many of the six million French-speaking Canadians who now live in Canada are descendants of the few thousand settlers who came to Quebec 350 years ago under the leadership of Samuel de Champlain.

ALSO READ: CANADA, EXPLORATION, QUEBEC.

CHANCE AND PROBABILITY
A farmer is ready to plant his field, but what should he plant? Hay will certainly grow, but he cannot make much money from it. He could make more money from corn, but corn will die if too little rain falls. He will then make no money at all. What should he do?

Whenever the outcome (result) of an event is not certain—when more than one result is possible—the event is called a *chance event*. The farmer's problem is a chance event—will enough rain fall for corn to grow? Many everyday events are chance events. Who will win the game? Will a tossed coin land "heads" or "tails"? Will the traffic light be green or red when you reach it?

The outcome of a chance event is uncertain, but we usually have some idea of which possible outcome is the most likely. The farmer, for example, could examine weather records to see if enough rain to grow corn usually falls in his area. If it doesn't, he should plant hay. If it does, he can take the risk and plant corn in his field.

Mathematicians have a way of calculating whetheı it is likely that an outcome will happen. This is called the *probability* of the event. A mathematician looks at all possible outcomes. He uses his experience and knowledge to tell which result is most likely to happen, or which result is most likely *not* to happen. Probability does not allow people to predict accurately what will happen in all instances. But if you use probability well, you can always make the best possible guess, and you will be right more often than wrong.

■ **LEARN BY DOING**

Here is a simple chance and probability situation. Put 5 red checkers and 10 black checkers into a box. Pull out one without looking. You can probably see that you have a better chance of picking a black checker than a red one. But how often will you pick a black one? You can find the probability by forming the fraction:

$$\frac{\text{Total of black checkers}}{\text{Total of all checkers}} = \frac{10}{15} = \frac{2}{3}$$

The probability ⅔ means that you will pick a black checker about 2 out of every 3 tries.

Probability works best over the long run, or on many tries. If you make 90 tries, you will probably pick about 60 black checkers, and you would probably pick about 600 black checkers in 900 tries. If you make only three tries, you *might* pick three red checkers. Keep a record of a large number of tries. What happens?

What is the probability that a tossed coin will land "heads" up? How many outcomes are possible for one coin toss? Make a number of tries and keep a record of the outcome. What happens when you toss two coins? Three? Keep tossing and see what happens. ■

ALSO READ: MATHEMATICS, MEASUREMENT, PERCENTAGE, STATISTICS.

CHAPLIN, CHARLIE (1889–1977) Throughout the world, the best known movie star has been the great comedian Charlie Chaplin. He created the little tramp who has great difficulty getting along with the world. The character was first seen in 1915 when British actor Charlie Chaplin played the part in the movie *The Kid Auto Races at Venice*. Chaplin made more than 70 silent movies

playing the part of "the tramp," with his little mustache, beat-up bowler hat, baggy trousers, enormous shoes, and stiff-legged walk. Everybody laughed and cried at the antics of the tramp.

Charles Spencer Chaplin was born in England. He came to the United States in 1910 as a comedian in a pantomime. He was asked to appear in the movies, and he became world famous five years later. He acted in his best-known short films, *The Floor Walker*, *One A.M.*, *Easy Street*, *The Pawnshop*, and *The Immigrant*, during 1916 and 1917. You may have seen on television some Charlie Chaplin reruns, such as *The Kid* (1920), *Gold Rush* (1925), and *Modern Times* (1936). *The Great Dictator*, made in 1940, was Chaplin's first talking movie.

In 1952, Chaplin settled in Switzerland with his wife, Oona, and his family. In 1972, a special Oscar was given to him, and in 1975, he was knighted by Queen Elizabeth II.

ALSO READ: ACTORS AND ACTING, MOTION PICTURES, PANTOMIME.

CHAPMAN, JOHN see APPLESEED, JOHNNY.

CHARIOT Machines of war can be traced back to the earliest chariots used by the Sumerians more than 4,000 years ago. Chariots were two-wheeled vehicles that were fast and

▲ *Charlie Chaplin gained worldwide fame as "the little tramp," the character he created. In the days of silent movies, he made people laugh without ever saying a word.*

▼ *The Egyptian pharaoh Tutankhamen in his chariot scatters his Syrian enemies. This scene is from a painted chest found in his tomb. It shows the effect that the chariot had on warfare in ancient Egypt.*

▲ *This golden bust of the emperor Charlemagne was made to hold parts of his skull after his death.*

easy to drive. They were usually pulled into battle by two horses, hitched side by side, although four horses were sometimes used. Chariots were small and light in weight. There was no seat, so the driver stood. Most chariots had room for only one or two people. Sheets of decorated metal were fastened around the front of the chariot to protect the driver in battle. The back was left open.

The armies of Mesopotamia and ancient Egypt often attached sharp curved blades to the chariot wheels to cut down attacking warriors. The Romans used chariots, but rarely in battle because they turned over too often when traveling over the rough countryside of western Europe. Instead, chariots became the symbol of victory in Roman parades and were used for races and games.

ALSO READ: CARRIAGE; EGYPT, ANCIENT; ROME, ANCIENT.

CHARLEMAGNE (742–814) Charlemagne was one of the greatest military leaders of the Middle Ages. His name in Latin means "Charles the Great." He earned this title by expanding the kingdom of the Franks into a huge empire. His empire included land that is today France, Italy, and Germany.

Charlemagne was the son of the Frankish king Pepin the Short and the grandson of Charles Martel. After Pepin's death, the Frankish kingdom was split between Charlemagne and his brother, Carloman. Charlemagne became ruler of the whole kingdom when Carloman died.

Charlemagne immediately began his wars of conquest. His first great military campaign was against the Lombards, who had invaded Italy and were threatening the pope. Charlemagne captured the Lombard kingdom and earned the valuable friendship of the pope. He defeated the Saxons in another important war

> Charlemagne learned to read, but it is probable that he couldn't write. He was a very big man, well over six feet tall.

and captured the northwest part of Germany. Pope Leo III crowned Charlemagne Emperor of the Romans on Christmas Day, 800. He made his capital city at Aachen, later called Aix-la-Chapelle.

Charlemagne was a strong and energetic ruler. He imposed a system of law and order on the many different people of his empire. He built schools and encouraged the work of artists and writers. But the government was very much under his personal control. After his death, the empire split up in chaos. Later, historians called him Charles I of the Holy Roman Empire.

ALSO READ: CHARLES MARTEL, FRENCH HISTORY, GERMAN HISTORY.

CHARLES, HOLY ROMAN EMPERORS The Holy Roman Empire was a union of German and Italian kingdoms established in A.D. 962. Seven rulers of the Holy Roman Empire were named Charles.

The Holy Roman Empire was sup-

▼ *Charles V ruled a larger empire than anyone since Charlemagne.*

posed to be a continuation of the empire of Charlemagne. So the emperors Charles I, Charles II, and Charles III were kings of France—Charlemagne, Charles the Bald, and Charles the Fat. Actually, the name Holy Roman Empire was not used until after the time of these three kings, but they were known as emperors anyway.

Charles IV (1316–1378) became king of Germany and Bohemia in 1346. He also ruled as Holy Roman Emperor after 1347. He issued an order, called the Golden Bull of 1356, which gave rules for the selection of future emperors.

Charles V (1500–1558) inherited a vast empire. Ferdinand and Isabella of Spain were his grandparents. So were the Holy Roman Emperor Maximilian I and Mary of Burgundy. He was left the Netherlands and Burgundy by his familiy. He became King of Spain in 1516 and was elected Holy Roman Emperor in 1519. Charles became the most important of all the Holy Roman emperors and ruled Spain at the height of its power.

Charles VI (1685–1740) became emperor after 1711. The other rulers of Europe agreed that if he did not have a son, his eldest daughter, Maria Theresa, would be his heir. When Charles died, the other rulers refused to let Maria Theresa inherit his lands. This started a long war.

Charles VII (1726–1745) was Holy Roman Emperor from 1742–45. Before becoming emperor, he was Charles Albert, a prince of Bavaria.

ALSO READ: CHARLEMAGNE; CHARLES, KINGS OF FRANCE; FRENCH HISTORY; HOLY ROMAN EMPIRE.

CHARLES, KINGS OF BRITAIN
Two British kings called Charles ruled over England, Scotland, and Ireland. There have also been two well-known British princes with that name.

Charles I (1600–1649), the son of King James I (the first King to rule both England and Scotland) came to the throne in 1625. He believed that God gave kings the right to rule, and he expected people to obey him blindly. This included worshiping God as he directed. But many of the English people refused to obey him. Charles quarreled again and again with Parliament, which represented the people.

Charles tried to rule without Parliament. But he found he could not legally raise any money without the agreement of the people. So he called Parliament back and tried to arrest members who would not obey his orders. Parliament, led by Oliver Cromwell, took control of the army and began a civil war in the name of the people's rights. Charles was defeated and beheaded. Cromwell then ruled Britain as Lord Protector.

Charles II (1630–1685) fought bravely for his father, Charles I, during the civil war. He fled to France after his father was beheaded. After Cromwell died in 1658, the people asked Charles to become king. He was crowned in 1660. Charles II is sometimes called the "Merry Monarch," because he liked pretty women

▲ *Charles II was a popular ruler—his first act as king was to pardon his enemies. He was also skillful enough to keep Parliament on his side.*

There were seven Holy Roman Emperors named Charles, the first of whom was Charlemagne. Eight other French kings, two kings of England, four kings of Spain, and 14 kings of Sweden also had the name Charles.

▼ *A woodcut of the 1600's showing the execution of Charles I.*

▲ *Charles and Diana, Prince and Princess of Wales, in a photo taken shortly after their wedding in 1981. The Royal Wedding in London was viewed on television by some 600 million people worldwide.*

▲ *Charles V of France, shown in an illuminated manuscript, being given a book (top) and hearing a lecture by a wise man (bottom).*

and elegant living. He encouraged the study of science and built up the navy. But, like his father, he wanted more money than Parliament would grant him. So he secretly accepted funds from the King of France.

Charles joined the Catholic Church but never forced his faith on others. Charles's wife had no children, so after he died his brother became King James II.

Princes *Charles Edward Stuart* (1720–1788) was called "Bonnie Prince Charlie." This grandson of James II was handsome, charming, and brave. The Stuart family, which had ruled England, Scotland, and Ireland since 1603, was no longer in power when he was born. Charles Edward made a gallant attempt in 1745 to recapture Britain for his family, but his forces were too weak to win the Battle of Culloden. The Scots hid him until he could escape.

Charles Philip Arthur George (born 1948), son of Queen Elizabeth II and Philip, Duke of Edinburgh, is the Prince of Wales and present heir to the British throne. He graduated from Cambridge University and the Royal Air Force College. From 1971 to 1976, Charles served in the Royal Navy. He married Lady Diana Spencer in July 1981.

ALSO READ: CROMWELL, OLIVER; ENGLISH HISTORY.

CHARLES, KINGS OF FRANCE

Ten kings of France were named Charles.

Charles I (823–877) was called "the Bald." (Historians also call him Charles II of the Holy Roman Empire). He was the grandson of Charlemagne. He and his two brothers fought over Charlemagne's empire. The Treaty of Verdun gave Charles the Bald the western part of the empire, and for the first time the area of France was a separate king-

dom. The people living there were called the Franks.

Charles II (839–888) was called "the Fat." (He was also Charles III of the Holy Roman Empire). He could not stop attacks on France by the Normans. His leading nobles removed him as king in 887.

Charles III (879–929) was called "the Simple." He gave the Normans land in what is now called Normandy. But he also gained land for France by taking over Lorraine. He was dethroned by his nobles after being king for 30 years.

Charles IV (1294–1328) was called "the Fair." He ruled for six years. He fought with King Edward II of England over English land that he claimed for France.

Charles V (1337–1380) was called "the Wise." He governed France as regent for several years while his father, John the Good, was held captive in England. He became king in 1364. He was almost successful in driving the English out of France for good. He did much for the arts, and founded the royal library.

Charles VI (1368–1422) was called "the Mad." He became king at the age of 12. He went insane at age 24. Civil war broke out over who should become the next king.

Charles VII (1403–1461) was called "the Victorious." He was the son of Charles VI. Joan of Arc helped to put him on the throne and helped him to defeat the English.

Charles VIII (1470–1498) was age 13 when he became king. Brittany became part of France during his reign. He also tried to conquer land in Italy, but he failed.

Charles IX (1550–1574) was just 10 years old when he became king. His mother, Catherine de Medici, governed during most of his reign.

Charles X (1757–1836) became king when the monarchy was restored after the French Revolution. He wanted to have as much power as the kings had before the revolution. The people revolted again, and Charles had to flee France.

ALSO READ: CHARLEMAGNE, FRENCH HISTORY, FRENCH REVOLUTION, HOLY ROMAN EMPIRE, HUNDRED YEARS' WAR, JOAN OF ARC.

CHARLES, JACQUES A. C. see BALLOON.

CHARLES MARTEL (688–741)

Charles Martel was the first ruler of the Franks, tribesmen who lived in the present-day France. He was also the grandfather of the famous emperor and soldier, Charlemagne, who ruled the first large European empire since the Romans.

Charles was called *Martel* ("hammer") because he was such a powerful fighter. His men compared Charles Martel to their war god, Thor, who was said to have always fought with a hammer.

In a very important battle near what is now Tours, France, Charles Martel defeated the invading Muslims in 732. The Arab, or Muslim, forces had invaded southern France from Spain. The Arabs expected to conquer easily the weak kings of the area and take control of all of western Europe. But Charles Martel raised a large cavalry and crushed the invaders at Tours in 732. The Arabs never again invaded western Europe after this defeat.

Charles Martel's title was actually Mayor of the Palace, but he had as much power as any king. He granted land to his nobles, starting the feudal system that continued throughout the Middle Ages. Under this system the noblemen who received land from him pledged to fight for him and to supply him with troops.

ALSO READ: BATTLES, FAMOUS; CHARLEMAGNE; FRENCH HISTORY; FEUDALISM; MIDDLE AGES.

CHAUCER, GEOFFREY (about 1340–1400)

"Whan that Aprille with his shoures sote / The droghte of March hath perced to the rote." ("When that April with its showers sweet/ The drought of March has pierced to the root.") These are the opening words of one of the greatest English poems ever written—*The Canterbury Tales* by Geoffrey Chaucer. They are written in Middle English—the English used in Chaucer's time.

Chaucer wrote his witty verse story 600 years ago. It is about 30 pilgrims on their way from London to the shrine of Thomas à Becket at Canterbury. Each pilgrim tells a story to pass the time. The pilgrims include all kinds of people—a knight, people of the church (a nun, a prioress, and a parson), a lawyer, a doctor, a sailor, a farmer, and a drunken miller. Chaucer pokes fun at many customs of his day in these stories.

Chaucer was the son of a well-to-do London wine merchant. He was a page in a prince's house as a boy and fought for his king, Edward III, in France. He was trusted with important government jobs throughout his life and represented England as a diplomat abroad. At home he was a justice of the peace and a member of Parliament. He was buried in Westminster Abbey in London.

ALSO READ: ENGLISH LANGUAGE, POETRY, WESTMINSTER ABBEY.

▲ *Charles Martel, first ruler of the Franks.*

Many phrases written by Chaucer are still used today: "brown as a berry," "every man for himself," "through thick and thin," "love is blind," "bless this house," and "it is no child's play."

◀ *Medieval pilgrims on their way to Canterbury. Chaucer wrote his* Canterbury Tales *around just such a group.*

CHECKERS Checkers is a very old game. Games similar to it were played thousands of years ago, and "modern" checkers began in the 1500's or before. Mathematicians have written books on how to win at checkers. It can be a very complicated game, but you and a friend can play it just for fun. You will need 12 red checkers, 12 black checkers, and a checkerboard. The board is divided into 64 squares, which are usually colored red and black. The checkers are placed on the black squares at the ends of the board, one on each black square in the three rows closest to each player.

The opening move is made by the player with black checkers. One of the checkers on the player's front row is moved forward one square *diagonally*, always staying on the black squares. The other player then moves a checker. The checkers move forward only, not backward.

The object of a checkers game is to capture all of your opponent's men. This is done by *jumping* them and removing them from the board. To jump one of your opponent's men, one of your checkers must be diagonally next to one of your opponent's, and the square diagonally behind the opponent's man must be empty. You capture the checker by lifting your checker over it, and placing your checker on the empty square. You can take two or more of your opponent's men with one jump, if you can keep moving forward and if one empty square lies between each of your opponent's men. You can win a game by forcing your opponent into a position where no moves can be made.

Try to make a *king* of one of your men by moving it onto the other player's back row. Your checker is then *crowned* by placing one of your captured checkers on top of the king. Kings give you an advantage, because they can move backward as well as forward.

CHEESE People have made and eaten cheese for many centuries. Cheese is eaten more frequently than meat in some parts of the world. Cheese contains nearly the same amounts of protein and other nutrients as the milk from which it is made. Ancient Greek athletes ate it to make themselves stronger. About 500 kinds of cheese are made, from mild cheese to strong-tasting and strong-smelling Limburger and Roquefort. But all cheese—mild or sharp—is made from milk. Most comes from the milk of cows. But milk from goats, sheep, llamas, reindeer, zebras, camels, buffaloes, and yaks is used in various parts of the world.

The basic process is the same for all cheeses. Milk is allowed to turn sour.

The United States produces more cheese than any other country— nearly five billion pounds per annum. The biggest cheese-eaters are the French. They consume more than 40 pounds (18kg) per person every year. There are 240 kinds of French cheese.

▼ *A checkerboard, showing (1) the board with the pieces in the starting position; (2) capturing a piece; (3) capturing several pieces by multiple jumps.*

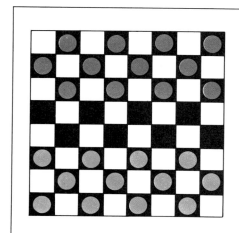

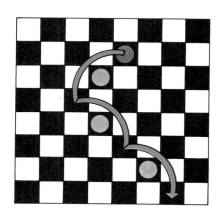

▲ *This large store of cheeses is in Switzerland, a country known for its fine dairy products.*

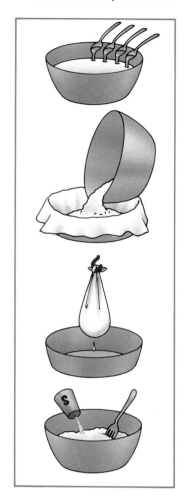

The white solid lumps, called *curd*, are used to make cheese. The yellowish liquid, or *whey*, is removed. Different cheeses are made from different kinds of milk or from mixtures of different kinds of milk.

Bacteria or another ingredient may be added to make curds more rapidly. Different cheeses may also be made by changing the amount of other ingredients, such as salt; raising or lowering the temperature the milk is kept at while curding; leaving some whey in the cheese or by taking out every drop; having different molds grow in the cheese; and *curing* (aging) the cheese for longer or shorter periods of time. The three main cheese groups are *soft* (such as cream cheese), *semisoft* (such as cottage cheese), and *hard* (such as Swiss cheese).

Years ago, cheese was made on individual farms, but now it is made mainly in factories. Two thirds of the cheese made in the United States comes from Wisconsin. New York makes about half the rest.

■ LEARN BY DOING

You can make cottage cheese, which is the first step in making any cheese. You will need a quart of sour milk. You can turn sweet milk sour in a few minutes by adding 4 teaspoons of vinegar to a quart of milk. Pour the sour milk into a piece of cheesecloth, which you can buy in a supermarket or hardware store. Tie the ends of the cloth together to make a bag, and hang the bag over a sink or bowl. Let it drip for a whole day. This removes all the whey. Untie the bag and pour the curds into a bowl. Sprinkle them with salt and mash with a fork. Put the cottage cheese into the refrigerator to chill. Try it with fruit or salad. ■

ALSO READ: BACTERIA, DAIRY PRODUCTS, FUNGUS.

CHEKHOV, ANTON (1860–1904)

The plays and short stories of the Russian writer Anton Chekhov are widely popular today. His works have been translated into many languages. Some of his plays have been made into films. Chekhov was the grandson of a freed serf (slave). Early in life he decided to be a doctor, and he won a scholarship to medical school. He started to write while practicing medicine. He created hundreds of short stories before turning to plays. His first major play was *The Seagull*. It was a failure at first, but in 1898 it was produced with great success by the Moscow Art Theater. Chekhov died of tuberculosis when he was only 44 years old.

The Cherry Orchard is probably Chekhov's best-known play. It tells the story of a noblewoman and her brother who are living in poverty. A friend suggests that they cut down their beloved cherry orchard for money, but they refuse. Sadly, their home and orchard are sold at auction to their so-called "friend." The last sound heard in the play is that of axes chopping down the cherry trees. *The Three Sisters* and *Uncle Vanya* are also among Chekhov's greatest plays. His work is sensitive as well as humorous. It hints at the downfall of the Russian upper class.

ALSO READ: DRAMA.

▲ *Anton Chekhov, great Russian author.*

CHEMICAL WEAPONS Burning sulfur, or some other choking chemical, to "smoke out" an enemy was an ancient form of chemical warfare. But it was not until World War I (1914–1918) that chemical weapons were used on a large scale. In 1915 the Germans attacked the Allies with poison gas. The gas floated over the Allied trenches, burning and choking the troops sheltered in them. Before World War I ended, both sides had used poison gas. Mustard gas, which caused huge blisters on the skin, put many soldiers out of action. Troops wore respirators ("gas masks") for protection.

Chemical weapons were never used in World War II. But during the Vietnam War, U.S. planes sprayed forests with chemicals, called *herbicides*, that killed the trees, in order to deny cover to the enemy. Chemical weapons can be fired from guns, sprayed from planes, or dropped as bombs. Some cause injuries; others can kill.

Almost everyone is frightened of chemical warfare. Soldiers practice wearing special suits for protection against poisonous chemicals, just in case these terrible weapons should ever be used.

ALSO READ: WORLD WAR I.

▼ Some of the more common items found in a chemistry laboratory are shown here. They are: (1) Chemical balance; (2) Bottles with ground glass stoppers; (3) Centrifuge; (4) Microscope; (5) Burette; (6) Conical flask; (7) Filter funnel; (8) Measuring cylinder; (9) Long-necked flask; (10) Pipette; (11) Flat-bottomed flask; (12) Beaker; (13) Test tube and holder; (14) Bunsen burner (15) Mortar and pestle; (16) Condenser; (17) Tripod stand.

CHEMISTRY Watch a log burn in a fireplace. Flames and smoke rise from the log. After a time, the flames go out, and there is no more smoke. The log has disappeared. In its place lies a pile of black and gray ashes. Changes have taken place in the log. The log was wood, but the ashes seem to be a material entirely different from wood. What materials make up the ashes, and what materials made up the wood? How can you tell these materials apart? And how did the log change to ashes? These are questions that chemistry can answer.

Modern chemists deal with many problems in many special situations. But all chemists are concerned with two main questions. (1) What is the make-up of all the substances in the world? (2) How can the make-up of a substance be changed?

Matter and Its Properties All materials are kinds of matter. *Matter* is anything that has weight and takes up space. You can see that a rock takes up space, and you learn that it has weight if you lift it. So a rock is one kind of matter. So is the paper this book is printed on, the hair on your head, a drinking glass and the water in it, the air in the room in which you are reading, and anything else you can see or feel.

A *property* is anything you can say about any kind of matter that helps you recognize it and tell it from other kinds of matter. A grain of sugar is white and solid. So is a grain of salt. Being white and being solid are two properties of both sugar and salt.

Sugar tastes sweet and salt tastes salty. Sweetness and saltiness are properties that enable you to tell sugar from salt. You can also tell salt from sugar if you look at the grains with a magnifying glass. Most salt grains are tiny cubes, but sugar grains are chunks. Thus the property of shape also helps you recognize salt and sugar.

Properties of matter are divided into two main kinds. (1) *Physical* properties include color, odor, taste, size, form or shape, melting temperature, boiling temperature, density (weight of each unit of volume), and state (solid, liquid, or gas). (2) *Chemical* properties include the ways different kinds of matter act when changing to other kinds of matter. Whether or not a material will burn is a chemical property. So is whether or not it will, like salt, dissolve in water.

Atoms and Elements   All matter is made up of extremely small particles called *atoms*. A row of 250 million average-size atoms, side by side, would be only one inch (2.5 cm) long. There are more than 100 different kinds of atoms. Matter made up of atoms of only one kind is called an *element*.

Chemists sometimes refer to elements by name, and sometimes by abbreviations, called *symbols*, of one or two letters. For example, H is the

▲ *In a laboratory, chemicals and equipment are arranged in an orderly fashion.*

Four million different chemical substances have been identified. This number keeps growing at a rate of over five thousand every week.

CHEMISTRY

CHEMICAL NAMES OF EVERYDAY SUBSTANCES

Aspirin
Sodium Acetyl Salicylate

Baking Soda
Sodium Bicarbonate

Battery Acid
Sulfuric Acid

Borax
Sodium Borate

Chalk
Calcium Carbonate

Common Salt
Sodium Chloride

Epsom Salts
Magnesium Sulfate

Lime
Calcium Oxide

Magnesia
Magnesium Oxide

Muriatic Acid
Hydrochloric Acid

Plaster of Paris
Calcium Sulfate

Saltpeter
Potassium Nitrate

Vinegar
Acetic Acid

Washing Soda
Sodium Carbonate

symbol for hydrogen, and Al is for aluminum. The symbols of some elements, such as Fe (iron) and Ag (silver), are abbreviations of the Latin names (*ferrum* and *argentum*) of these elements. (See the list of known elements and their symbols with the article on ELEMENT.)

Molecules and Compounds Atoms of the same element or of different elements can be joined, or combined. Oxygen is a gas made up of oxygen atoms joined in pairs. Other gases made up of paired atoms are hydrogen, nitrogen, chlorine, and fluorine. Atoms joined into pairs or larger groups are called *molecules*. Paired oxygen atoms are oxygen molecules. A chemist would write O_2 for "a molecule of oxygen." The "$_2$" means that the molecule contains two atoms.

Most molecules are not made up of atoms of the same element, but rather of different elements. Two atoms of hydrogen joined to one atom of oxygen make up one molecule of water. A chemist would show a water molecule as H_2O. This combination of symbols is called a *formula*. It is easy to see that water has properties quite different from the elements that make it up. Hydrogen is a *gas* that will burn. Oxygen is a *gas* that supports burning. Water is a *liquid* that does not burn.

Materials made up of more than one element are called *compounds*. From this you can see that the smallest possible part of a compound is a single molecule. Also, a molecule is the smallest part of a compound that has the properties of the compound. Water is a compound. If you break apart the atoms that make up a water molecule, you get the gases of which the water was made, not pieces of a water molecule. Most compounds are made up of molecules that have more than two atoms. Some have hundreds. Chemists have discovered or made over a million chemical compounds.

Physical and Chemical Changes
Put a few ice cubes into a teakettle, and put the kettle at low heat on a stove. The ice (a solid) soon melts, changing to water (a liquid). Then, after a time, the water boils, becoming steam (a gas), which appears as a clear space just in front of the spout.

Water in the form of a solid (ice) changed to a liquid (water), and then to a gas (steam) in this experiment. The changes all were *changes of state*, a physical property. Changes in the physical properties of matter are *physical changes*. The make-up of the water remained the same throughout these physical changes. The water molecules remained unchanged—two atoms of hydrogen and one of oxygen.

■ LEARN BY DOING

An eggshell is made up of the solid compound, calcium carbonate, which chemists write $CaCO_3$. Vinegar is mostly made up of the liquid compound acetic acid, $H_4C_2O_2$. Break an eggshell into small pieces. Put six or eight pieces into a drinking glass, and pour in vinegar (white vinegar is best) to a depth of about an inch (2.5 cm). Bubbles will rise from the pieces of eggshell. The bubbles are carbon dioxide, CO_2, a gas made up of one atom of carbon and two of oxygen. If you could analyze the vinegar, you would find that a compound called calcium acetate, $CaH_6C_4O_4$, had been formed. The carbon dioxide and calcium acetate are very unlike the eggshell and vinegar. The new compounds are the results of a *chemical change*, one in which the molecules of matter exchange atoms, making new compounds. ■

Chemical changes, or *reactions*, occur everywhere around us. Food undergoes changes in cooking, as well as in the bodies of the living things that eat it. Batteries produce electricity by means of chemical changes. Rust on iron and tarnish on silver are caused by chemical changes, too.

■ LEARN BY DOING

You can produce—and remove—the blackish stain called tarnish. Place some cooked egg yolk on a sterling silver spoon for half an hour or so. The spoon will be tarnished wherever it touched the egg. Tarnish is a chemical called silver sulfide, made of silver (from the spoon) and sulfur (from the egg).

Soap and water will not clean the spoon. The tarnish must be changed *back* to two separate chemicals, silver and sulfur. Household silver polish will do this easily, or you can make silver polish yourself. Pour 2 cups of water into an aluminum pot (*only* aluminum will work). Add ½ teaspoon of salt and ½ teaspoon of baking soda. Boil the liquid and gently slide the spoon into it. Wait two or three minutes, *carefully* take out the spoon, and wash it in cool water. The tarnish will have disappeared—another chemical change! ■

The Development of Chemistry

Ancient people took the hair off animal hides by rubbing them with a paste made of wood ashes and water. They made wine from berries and fruits, and made dyes, soap, bronze, and other things that required the use of chemistry. But these people had no idea of chemistry nor that they were using it.

In the Middle Ages, men called *alchemists* believed they could find the philosopher's stone, a material that would turn cheap metals, such as lead, into gold. This search was a failure, but alchemists discovered a number of things about matter and how it acts, which later gave people the facts they needed to establish the science of chemistry.

European experiments made chemistry a science in the 1600's and 1700's. The English, Germans, Swedes, Scots, and French all took part. Accurate measurement, one of the most important parts of science, was applied to the study of matter and

▲ *Artificial fibers are made from chemicals. Above, viscose rayon filaments leave the acid bath and are wound up on a rotating wheel before joining the other fibers.*

its changes. And the idea of chemical compounds was put forth.

At the beginning of the 1800's, the idea of atoms and molecules was proposed. By the end of the 1800's, this idea had become the basis of chemistry. Chemistry also became an important industry in the 1800's, and beginning late in that century, chemists learned how to produce an ever-increasing number of useful products.

Chemists are constantly devising new chemical changes and using known ones to make new, useful things. Chemists today make artificial fibers such as rayon, nylon, Orlon, and Dacron, which can be used in place of cotton and wool. Chemists have made medicines, such as antibiotics and sulfa drugs, that have conquered many diseases.

Large chemical industries have grown up in many countries. Scientists and engineers use chemistry to make a great number of things for people to buy and other industries to use. The chemical industry in the United States employs nearly a million workers.

For quite a while in the 1800's, chemists had one main job—taking things apart. Chemists discovered what chemicals, and how much of each chemical, were in a certain substance. Then chemists slowly learned how to put things together. Some

The human body contains many different chemicals. More than half the atoms in your body are hydrogen, the simplest element. Next in abundance is oxygen. Then comes carbon, making up one-tenth of the body's weight. That is enough, if it were in pure carbon form, to fill 3,000 "lead" pencils.

Chemical balances are so sensitive that they can weigh a person's name written on paper with a pencil.

chemists learned how to *synthesize* (produce) natural substances in the laboratory. Other chemists began to produce things that never existed in nature. Chemists turned to the makeup of the atom itself and began to study what happens to a substance when the nuclei of its atoms are changed. Today, the work of chemists is closely related to the work of physicists. Their work also takes them into the fields of astronomy, biology, and other natural sciences.

For further information on:
Chemical Processes and Properties, *see* ABSORPTION, BLEACHING, DIGESTION, DISTILLATION, ENERGY, FIRE.
Chemical and Chemical Products, *see* ACIDS AND BASES, AEROSOL, ALLOY, BATTERY, CARBON, DYE, ELEMENT, EXPLOSIVES, FIRE EXTINGUISHER, FIREWORKS, FUEL, GAS, GASOLINE, HYDROGEN, INK, MATCH, NITROGEN, OXYGEN, PAINT, PERFUME, PLASTIC, RUBBER, SALT, SOAPS AND DETERGENTS, SYNTHETICS.
Forms of Matter, *see* ATOM, CRYSTAL, ELEMENT, GAS, LIQUID, MATTER, METAL, SOLID, WATER.
History, *see* ALCHEMY; BACON, ROGER; CURIE FAMILY; FARADAY, MICHAEL; LAVOISIER, ANTOINE; PASTEUR, LOUIS; PHYSICS; PRIESTLEY, JOSEPH.

CHENG HO Imagine a fleet of 300 sailing ships exploring unknown seas. Such great expeditions set out from China in the 1400's. They were commanded by a bold and skillful leader, Cheng Ho.

Cheng Ho led seven voyages between 1404 and 1433. He was told by the Chinese emperor to explore the "western oceans." The Chinese visited Vietnam, India, Arabia, and Egypt. They even reached the coast of Africa. Everywhere the ships dropped anchor, Cheng Ho summoned the local people and told them they must respect and obey the power of the great Chinese emperor.

At the time of Cheng Ho's voyages, no European sailors had ever seen Asia. By the time European explorers sailed across the Indian Ocean to Asia, the Chinese had already explored the trade routes.

ALSO READ: CHINA, EXPLORATION.

CHEROKEE INDIANS When Europeans first came to America, the Cherokee Indians were living in villages and farming the fertile mountain valleys in what are now North and South Carolina, Tennessee, Georgia, and Alabama.

The Cherokees adopted many European ways. They learned to farm and raise animals in the same way the colonists did. During the Revolutionary War, the Cherokee took the British side against the Americans. Later, they developed a form of government like that of the United States and called themselves the Cherokee Nation. In 1821 a Cherokee chief named

▼ *A portrait in oil from the 1700's of a Cherokee chieftain dressed in a mixture of Indian and European costume.*

Sequoyah invented an alphabet for writing the Cherokee language. Almost everyone in the tribe learned to read and write. They started to print their own newspaper in 1828. The Cherokee Nation also had a public school system.

Like other eastern Indians, the Cherokees were pushed westward by the new settlers. The Cherokees gave up a big portion of their land to the federal government in 1785. The government promised they could keep the rest of the land, but settlers continued to trespass. Gold was discovered on Cherokee land in 1829. The Cherokees tried to protect their homeland, but the U.S. government ordered their removal.

During the winter of 1838–1839, U.S. troops forced about 15,000 Cherokee men, women, and children to move westward to Indian Territory. Almost 4,000 Cherokees died of hunger, exposure, and disease on this 1,000-mile (1,600-km) forced march, called later the "Trail of Tears." Those who survived became one of the Five Civilized Tribes that settled in the territory that later became Oklahoma. Today, some 24,000 Cherokees or part-Cherokees live in Oklahoma; about 6,000 still live in western North Carolina.

ALSO READ: INDIANS, AMERICAN; OKLAHOMA; SEQUOYAH.

CHESAPEAKE BAY The irregular shoreline of the Chesapeake Bay cuts 195 miles (314 km) into the eastern coast of the United States. The bay borders one side of the Delmarva Peninsula. The peninsula holds Maryland's "eastern shore," the state of Delaware, and part of Virginia. Thus the name—Delmarva.

Several rivers flow into the bay. The largest are the York, Rappahannock, Potomac, Susquehanna, and James. Plantations that date back to days before the American Revolution

▲ *The waters of Chesapeake Bay sparkle in the late afternoon light as an oyster dredge makes its way back to port.*

stand along the sheltered shores of the bay.

"Chesapeake" comes from American Indian words meaning "land of a great expanse of water." Indians took advantage of the plentiful shellfish there, and gathering oysters and crabs still remains big business on the bay. Oysters are becoming less plentiful, however, because water pollution by industry is killing them.

Oceangoing ships can travel almost the entire length of the Chesapeake Bay. Ships carry cargo to Baltimore, Maryland, near the head of the bay. Baltimore ranks as the thirteenth busiest seaport in the United States. Norfolk and Newport News, Virginia, stand near the entrance to the bay. The U.S. Navy maintains a base near Norfolk. Newport News has shipyards where some of the world's largest ships have been built.

For a long time, the bay was a barrier to land transportation. Now a highway bridge carries automobiles across the upper bay, near Annapolis, Maryland. At the bay entrance, the Chesapeake Bay Bridge-Tunnel crosses more than 17½ miles (28 km) of water to Cape Charles and Cape Henry in Virginia.

ALSO READ: CLAMS AND OYSTERS, DELAWARE, JAMESTOWN, MARYLAND, SEACOAST, VIRGINIA.

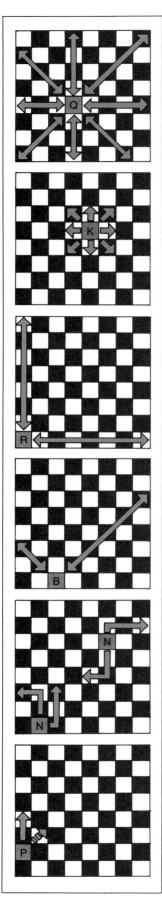

CHESS To play chess well, you must have skill, patience, and the ability to plan your moves before you make them. But even if you are just starting to learn the game, you can have fun playing it.

Chess is like a game of war between two kingdoms. The players sit opposite each other at a chessboard, a checkered board with 64 squares. One of the players uses the white (or light-colored) pieces, or chessmen, while the other uses the black (or dark-colored) ones. Each has 16 pieces—one *king*, one *queen*, two *rooks* (or *castles*), two *bishops*, two *knights*, and eight *pawns*. The picture shows where each piece is placed at the start of a game. Notice that the white king is on a black square. Across the board from the white king, the black king is on a white square.

The object of chess is to force your opponent's king to surrender. You and your opponent use your men to protect your king and to attack the enemy king. When a piece is moved onto a square occupied by an enemy piece, the enemy piece is *captured* and removed from the board. When the king is in danger of being captured, it is in *check* and must be moved out of

◀ *Chess pieces on a chess board and the moves that can be made with each piece.*

check or protected. The game ends when the king cannot move to safety or be protected from capture. This is *checkmate*. When neither player can win, the game is *drawn*.

Movement of the Pieces Each type of chess piece is moved in a different way. The queen is the most powerful piece. You can move it clear across the board in one turn. The queen can go forward, backward, to the right or left, or diagonally, any number of squares, if there are no other pieces in its path. The king can also move in any direction—but only one square at a time. Capture of the king ends the game. The rooks, or castles, move forward or backward, right or left, any number of squares, but never diagonally. The bishops move diagonally any number of squares. Pawns move forward one square at a time. But a player may advance a pawn two squares the first time it is moved. The pawn can move one square diagonally only to capture another piece. It can never move backward or sideways. A pawn that crosses the board is promoted. It is then exchanged for any other piece except a king. An upside-down rook or a coin is used to mark this piece. A player can, therefore, have two or more queens, bishops, knights, or rooks on the board, but never more than one king. A pawn is

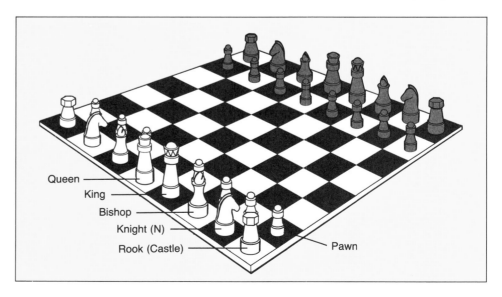

Queen
King
Bishop
Knight (N)
Rook (Castle)
Pawn

▲ *Players concentrate during an international chess tournament.*

usually made into a queen because a queen is so strong. This process of promoting is known as *queening a pawn.*

The knights move in an L-shape. A knight can go two squares forward, backward, or to either side, and then one square to the right or left. It can also go one square in any direction, and then two squares to the right or left. The knight is the only piece that can jump over other pieces when it moves.

Once you know how the pieces are moved, the trick is to know where to move them. Look around the board to see if any of your pieces are in danger of being captured as you advance toward the enemy. You especially do not want your queen to be captured. Make sure you do not leave your king unprotected. Toward the end of a chess game, the players usually have only a few men left, because the others have been captured. The game becomes very exciting, because the weak king is often left to defend itself.

History of Chess Chess was played thousands of years ago. A chess set was discovered in the tomb of an ancient Egyptian pharaoh. The game reached Persia and Arabia in the A.D. 500's. The word "chess" comes from the Persian word *shah*, meaning "king." Arab traders probably introduced chess to Western Europe, and European colonists later brought it

with them to America. People all over the world play chess today. Many countries have national tournaments. One of the most famous American players is Bobby Fischer. He won his first national championship in 1958, when he was 14 years old. He was named one of the world's most skillful players later the same year. International tournaments are held regularly, with players from many nations competing for the title of world champion. In recent years, most of the winners have been from the Soviet Union. The 1986 world championship was won by Gary Kasparov playing against Anatoly Karpov in a match played half in London, England and half in Leningrad, U.S.S.R.

CHIANG KAI-SHEK (1886–1975)

Chiang Kai-shek was the head of the government of the Republic of China (Taiwan). He gained fame as one of the four Allied military leaders of World War II.

Chiang was born in the province of Chekiang, China. He received his education in military schools in China and Japan. He met Dr. Sun Yat-sen, "father of the Chinese Republic," in Tokyo and joined the movement for revolt against the Manchus, who then ruled China.

Chiang worked for the political party that overthrew the Manchu dynasty and proclaimed China a republic. Chiang took command of the Nationalist army after Sun's death in 1925. He established the government at Nanking two years later. That same year, he married Soon Mei-ling, who became well known as her husband's close adviser.

Chiang was kidnapped in 1936 by General Chang and other army officers who wanted to make a strong defense against Japan, which had taken some Chinese territory. But Chou En-lai, a Communist, brought about Chiang's release. Chiang led

There are more than 170 septillion different ways of playing the 10 opening moves in a game of chess. (A septillion has 24 zeros!)

▲ *Chiang Kai-shek, who was the major leader of China from the 1920's to the end of World War II.*

It is perhaps fitting that Chicago should have the world's tallest building, the Sears Tower. The first modern skyscraper was built in Chicago in 1885. It was called the Home Insurance Building.

both the Nationalist and Communist armies against Japan.

Chiang was the major leader of China until the closing days of World War II. The Communists then began a civil war that drove Chiang's Nationalists from the mainland to the island of Taiwan off the coast of China. At Taipei, Taiwan, Chiang set up the government of the Republic of China in 1950. He reorganized his military forces, with the goal of regaining power over all China. He ruled until his death in 1975.

ALSO READ: CHINA, SUN YAT-SEN, TAIWAN, WORLD WAR II.

CHICAGO   Chicago, Illinois, is the third largest city in the United States and the business capital of the Midwest. Nearly eight million persons live in and around the city.

Chicago owes its importance to geography. It is at the south end of Lake Michigan, and land traffic must detour around the lake through the city. The plains to the east, south, and west of Chicago are rich farmlands.

Chicago has also become a world port. Oceangoing ships have sailed right up to city docks since the opening of the St. Lawrence Seaway, which connects the Great Lakes and the Atlantic Ocean through the St. Lawrence River.

Before the American Revolution, a trading post was opened at the southern end of Lake Michigan. It was started by Jean Baptiste Pointe du Sable (1745–1818), a black sailor, son of an African slave and a French merchant. Fort Dearborn grew up around the post. It was the scene of a tragic Indian massacre during the War of 1812.

As American settlers pushed west from the Atlantic coast, Chicago developed quickly. In 1871, according to legend, a cow kicked over a lantern. The fire that resulted wiped out almost the entire city. Only a stone water tower remained. Within a few years, the city had been rebuilt larger than ever. The first skyscraper was constructed in Chicago in 1885. It was ten stories high.

The city is a great industrial, agricultural, and financial center. It is an important rail and highway hub. Chicago's O'Hare International Airport is the busiest in the world. Among the city's chief landmarks are the Sears Tower, the world's tallest skyscraper, and the Merchandise Mart, the world's biggest commercial building. The city has outstanding museums of art, history, and science, as well as a superb symphony orchestra. The University of Chicago and other institutions of higher learning make the city an educational center.

ALSO READ: CITY, ILLINOIS.

CHICKEN   see POULTRY.

CHICKEN POX   see CHILDHOOD DISEASES.

▼ *Traffic moves at a crawl as a train speeds by overhead in Chicago, the third largest U.S. city. Like many large city centers, Chicago is working to solve problems caused by overcrowding.*

CHILD CARE A child at different ages needs different kinds of care. As a child grows older, the parents change their ways of looking after and caring for him or her.

What the Infant Needs When a baby is very young, he cannot do anything for himself—not even turn over. His mother soon learns what sounds he makes when he is hungry. She gives him his milk when he wants it. She changes his diapers every few hours and makes sure that he is warm enough. The family is careful to see that a cold draft does not blow on him and the sun does not shine directly into his eyes. The baby should be turned over from time to time so that he will not get too tired of one position. His wobbly head should be held carefully when he is picked up. He must never be left alone in a bathtub because he might drown. His family protects him from loud noises that frighten him and make him feel uneasy.

From the time he is born, a baby needs to feel that he is loved. He does not understand words yet, but he knows if he is loved by the way people treat him. If he is picked up only when he must be changed or fed, if he is handled quickly and roughly, or if

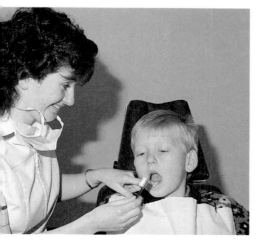

▼ *Regular visits to the dentist are part of caring for our teeth to prevent problems later on.*

the voices he hears sound impatient, it will be hard for him to feel he is really wanted. But if he is picked up lovingly and held in warm arms, if he is stroked and rocked, and if the voices around him are gentle, he will feel that he is wanted very much. It is important for a child to feel loved. It makes all the other things he must learn much easier, both in school and at play with his friends.

What the Young Child Needs As the baby grows bigger, he will be awake longer and want people around him. Brothers and sisters can be a special help at this time. They can amuse the baby by winding up his toys, picking up the toys he drops, and playing peek-a-boo with him. When he is old enough to crawl about the house, someone must watch over him whenever he is awake to see that he does not put small objects in his mouth, hurt himself on sharp edges of furniture, or fall down the stairs. It is much more work to take care of a crawling baby than a tiny infant. A child wants to do more things for himself.

What All Children Need Taking care of a child means making sure that he has the right kinds of food, the proper clothes, and enough sleep and exercise. It means regular visits to the doctor and dentist so that his body and teeth will stay healthy. And it means teaching him how to get along with other people, how to share toys with his playmates and to be patient. He learns these things best by watching the other members of his family. If they often shout and quarrel and find fault with the things he does, there is a good chance he will learn to fight with other children. But if the members of his family treat each other fairly and praise him for the things he can do, he will pass this love and security on to other people and will treat them as he has been treated.

Most of all, a child of any age needs

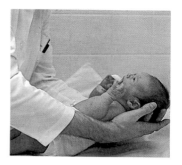

▲ *The muscles of a young baby's neck are not yet strong enough to support his head.*

▲ *A newborn baby is totally dependent on his parents to feed and comfort him. Most of his time is spent eating or sleeping. He sleeps with his hands still tightly curled, as they were inside his mother before he was born.*

A baby usually cannot catch a disease for about three months after he is born. This is because he has inherited immunity from his mother. The mother's disease-fighting substances are passed on to her baby. This gives the baby's body time to form its own fighting substances against some diseases.

to feel that he is loved just because he is himself, and not because he gets good grades in his school work or is a good ball player or does as he is told. Each child is like all other children in some ways and different in some ways. He is happiest when his parents let him take as long as he needs to learn each new thing.

ALSO READ: EDUCATION, GROWTH, LEARNING, NUTRITION.

CHILDHOOD DISEASES Some diseases infect children more often than adults, so they are known as childhood diseases. These illnesses are *contagious*, so that if one child becomes ill, it is possible that children he or she sits near at school or plays with will get the disease, too. Having a childhood disease usually leaves a child with an *immunity*—that is, he or she won't get it again. Today children can be made immune to several childhood diseases by being vaccinated. *Vaccines* contain killed or weakened viruses or bacteria. Vaccines are given by injection or by mouth. Adults sometimes get childhood diseases and may become more ill than children having the same ailment.

The childhood diseases usually include chicken pox, measles, German measles (rubella), mumps, whooping cough, scarlet fever, diphtheria, and polio. A test for possible tuberculosis is given to young children.

Chicken pox is very easily passed from one child to another. A rash breaks out two or three weeks after a child is exposed to the virus. This rash develops into itchy spots that are soon filled with a clear fluid. A red area sometimes stands out sharply around each spot. It is important not to scratch these spots, for they become infected easily and may leave scars. Presently a vaccine to prevent chicken pox is being developed.

Measles and *German measles* (*rubella*) are similar in name, but quite different as diseases. Measles usually lasts seven to ten days. It is more serious for the child, producing severe fever, rash, and possible ear infection and pneumonia. German measles may be mild in children, who might not even feel sick. But it can be dangerous to a mother who is in her first three months of pregnancy, because this disease can attack her unborn child, producing deafness, mental retardation, blindness, or heart disease. There is a vaccine which can be given to prevent measles and German measles.

Mumps is another childhood disease for which there is a vaccine. The mumps virus causes the glands to swell under the jawbone and the ears, so that swallowing is difficult and painful.

Whooping cough, *scarlet fever*, and *diphtheria* are caused by bacteria rather than viruses. A high temperature and a sore throat are typical of scarlet fever. So is a bright red skin rash that lasts about a week. Diphtheria is a more serious disease. The throat becomes inflamed and swollen. A membrane forms in the throat that can block a person's breathing. Whooping cough resembles a cold at first, but a nasty cough develops. The affected person coughs several times, then takes a deep, gasping breath. This produces a whooping sound from which the disease gets its name. Fortunately, there are vaccines for whooping cough and diphtheria, and antibiotics can be given for cases of scarlet fever.

Just a generation ago, parents were afraid that their children might catch *poliomyelitis* (polio). This disease, which starts with fever and muscle pains, can cause lifetime paralysis of leg, arm, or other muscles in a few days. But the disease will never threaten the United States again if children are vaccinated on schedule. The Sabin vaccine, which can be swallowed, is used today to prevent polio.

CHICKEN POX

How caught Direct contact, breathing germs

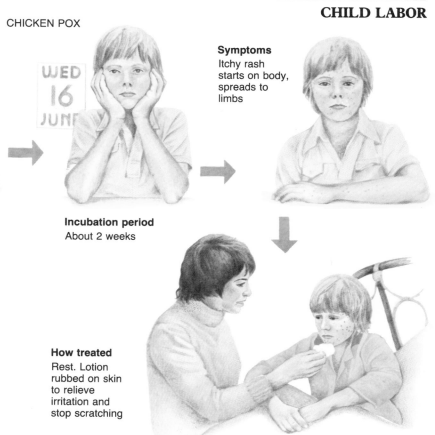

Symptoms
Itchy rash
starts on body,
spreads to
limbs

Incubation period
About 2 weeks

▲ *Chicken pox is easily caught from someone already infected. The incubation period is before the symptoms appear.*

How treated
Rest. Lotion
rubbed on skin
to relieve
irritation and
stop scratching

■ LEARN BY DOING

The table on this next page shows a schedule for getting vaccinations and tuberculin (tuberculosis) testing for babies and children recommended by the association of children's doctors in the United States (the American Academy of Pediatrics). Ask your parents which of these vaccines you have had. Perhaps you have a card from a baby clinic that gave you important vaccinations when you were very small. Which ones should you have this year? Which ones will come next year? Are there any you have *not* had but should? Your parents and teachers would like to be reminded about them. If every child had vaccinations on a regular schedule, most childhood diseases would disappear from the world. ■

ALSO READ: CONTAGIOUS DISEASES, DISEASE, IMMUNITY.

CHILD LABOR In every age of human history, children have had some chores to do. Sometimes it was just helping around the house. Sometimes it was building fires. Sometimes it was hunting and trapping. Later on, children were taught trades. They were apprenticed to weavers, carpenters, printers, and other craftsmen. They were expected to enter similar work on their own after several years spent learning a trade. But in the

CHILDHOOD DISEASES			
Age At Which Shots Are Usually Given.	**Diseases**	**Have You Had This Vaccination?**	
		YES	NO
2 months	DPT (D = diphtheria; P = pertussis—whooping cough; T = tetanus) OPV = oral (by mouth) polio vaccine; S = smallpox	☐	☐
4 months	DPT–OPV	☐	☐
6 months	DPT	☐	☐
12 months	Tuberculin test Live Measles vaccine	☐ ☐	☐ ☐
15–18 months	DPT–OPV-S-MMR (M = Measles; M = Mumps; R = Rubella—German Measles)	☐	☐
4–8 years	DPT- OPV, preferably at or before entry to school	☐	☐
14–16 years	Td—contains the same dose of tetanus toxoid as DPT and a reduced dose of diphtheria toxoid	☐	☐
Thereafter	Repeat Td every 10 years throughout life	☐	☐

HAVE YOU BEEN VACCINATED AGAINST ALL THE CHILDHOOD DISEASES?

▲ *The demand for factory workers during the Industrial Revolution meant that children and women worked long hours, often in dangerous, dirty conditions.*

In the United States today, more than five million children between the ages of 14 and 18 do some work at some time during the year, but this work is carefully controlled in all 50 states.

1800's the question of child labor became a problem that worried many people.

The Industrial Revolution developed rapidly in England in the early 1800's. Machines began to be used to manufacture products. Busy factories, mills, and mines needed more and more people to work in them. Owners of cotton mills collected poor children and orphans from throughout the kingdom to work in the mills. The mill owners paid for the children's food and shelter.

Children, some as young as five years of age, had to work up to 16 hours a day. The machines injured and crippled many, and young people became sick or died from the terrible working conditions. Charles Dickens wrote about the dreadful situation in his book, *David Copperfield*. People finally began to be concerned and set out to do something about the matter. The first labor law protecting the rights of children was passed in Britain in 1802.

In the United States, the first laws concerning child labor were passed in Massachusetts in 1842. In 1848 Pennsylvania set a minimum age of 12 years old for children working in mills. These laws stated the number of hours children could work and required children to attend school. The law that finally ended child labor abuses in the United States was the Fair Labor Standards Act passed in 1938. This was a federal law. It stated that children had to be at least 16 to work in jobs involving trade among states. Later changes said they could not work at dangerous jobs until they were 18 but allowed children of 14 to work at some jobs that did not harm schooling or health.

Today, children's working conditions are carefully regulated by law in the United States, Canada, Great Britain, and other countries. However, in Asia, Africa, and other parts of the world, boys and girls work long hours at dangerous jobs. There is

little or no control over their working conditions. The International Labor Organization, an agency of the United Nations, is working to control child labor.

ALSO READ: INDUSTRIAL REVOLUTION.

CHILDREN'S GAMES Children play hundreds of different games, games for a group and games for one child, indoor games and outdoor games, quiet games and noisy games. Some games are very active, but others don't require much energy. Different variations of the same game can be found around the world.

Many persons believe that games or play are the "work" of children. These are scientists, called *psychologists*, who think that games provide a training ground where children learn skills needed or useful to them in adulthood.

Learning to share responsibility and working together are very important in group games such as Tug of War. Making quick decisions and acting on those decisions are essential in games such as Red Light and Tag. The ability to follow someone and take directions is emphasized in Follow the Leader and Capture the Flag. Most games emphasize qualities such as teamwork, dependability, and unselfishness.

The most common games involve competition. Many of these types of games are sports that children can play throughout their lives. Such games or sports include baseball, tennis, ping-pong, checkers, chess, and charades.

Games have been played by children for thousands of years. They have been played for amusement and for training children how to survive. Some children of African tribes and aborigines of Australia still play games with spears, bow and arrows, and boomerangs that teach skills of hunting for food. South American

Indian children play games making traps and snares that will be used to hunt for food.

ALSO READ: CARD GAMES, CHARADES, CHECKERS, CHESS, SPORTS.

CHILDREN'S LITERATURE

Books take you to faraway places and to lands of make-believe. They teach many things and help a person grow. You learn how to read when you start school. Soon you will be able to read the great classics of literature.

Early Books Storytellers, and children to listen to them, have probably been around as long as people have. Myths, legends, fables, fairy stories, and folk tales have been handed down from generation to generation by word of mouth from the earliest times. But books just for children were first written only about 400 years ago. One of the earliest "books" for young people was the European *hornbook* of the 1500's. A hornbook was a small, paddle-shaped piece of wood with a piece of paper glued to it. The alphabet, the numerals, and usually the Lord's Prayer were printed on the paper. A thin sheet of clear horn covered the paper to protect it because paper was very expensive. Many hornbooks were tied around their owner's necks, so that the valuable printing and the paper would not be lost. The *chapbook*, a little magazine containing stories and rhymes, became popular in England in the 1600's.

The first picture book for children was published in 1657. It was the *Orbis Sensualium Pictus*, or "The World in Pictures," by John Amos Comenius, a Moravian writer. It taught natural history and was illustrated with woodcuts. This book, and most other books of the 1600's, were not meant for fun. Many of these books were written by Christian ministers and were full of *morals* (lessons

on how to behave) and grim warnings about what would happen to children who did not learn—and obey—the lessons. *The New England Primer*, printed in 1690 in the Massachusetts Bay Colony, was such a "teaching" book. The Puritans, both in England and in the American colonies, looked upon children as small adults. Children were taught always to behave like grown-ups.

New Ideas But French writers of the 1600's knew that children would like some fun now and then. A Frenchman called Charles Perrault wrote fairy tales especially for children, including *Cinderella*, *Beauty and the Beast*, *Bluebeard*, *Sleeping Beauty*, and *Red Riding Hood*. They were printed in English in the early 1700's by a London publisher, John Newbery. Newbery published many books just for children, including the "Mother Goose" nursery rhymes and *The History of Little Goody Two Shoes*. A medal named after him is given in the United States each year to the author of the best book for children. One of Newbery's assistants invented a kind of book called the *battledore*. It was a three-part piece of cardboard, printed with numbers, letters, and stories. Battledores had illustrations.

Some books interest both children and adults. The English writer Jonathan Swift wrote *Gulliver's Travels* (1726). It tells about some faraway, imaginary lands where people are very big and very tiny and speak unusual languages. But the story is not just one of make-believe. It is also a criticism of English society and government.

Jean Jacques Rousseau, a French philosopher, published a book called *Émile* in 1762. In it he explained his ideas about a new method of teaching. Rousseau believed that children should be taught as children, not as though they were small adults. His ideas helped greatly to make children's books—and education itself—

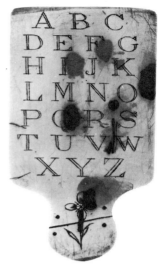

▲ *A hornbook of the 1500's.*

▼ *An illustration for one of the most famous Mother Goose rhymes, "Polly Put the Kettle On." It is drawn in the style of Kate Greenaway, who created many charming illustrations for children's rhymes and stories in the 1800's.*

▲ *A page from Kate Greenaway's* Birthday Book for Children.

▼ *Lewis Carroll's* Alice in Wonderland *is still a classic of children's literature. John Tenniel, who provided illustrations such as the one below for the book, became almost as famous as its author.*

more entertaining and less strict. But books that children liked were not published regularly until the 1800's. Writers and poets began to think about how children really feel, not how grown-ups think children should feel.

Books Begin to Be Fun Charles Lamb and his sister Mary rewrote the plays of Shakespeare for children in the early 1800's. Nathaniel Hawthorne retold Greek myths in a simple, enjoyable way. The brothers Jakob and Wilhelm Grimm produced *Grimm's Fairy Tales*, including *Rapunzel* and *Hansel and Gretel*. Washington Irving used the Dutch legends of New York State in stories such as *The Legend of Sleepy Hollow*, in which the timid Ichabod Crane has a spooky run-in with the Headless Horseman. The Grimms' friend, Hans Christian Andersen, wrote wonderful children's stories such as *The Ugly Duckling* and *The Steadfast Tin Soldier*. Andrew Lang collected charming folk tales from all over the world for the *Blue Fairy Tale Book*, the first of a treasured series.

During this same period, Lewis Carroll wrote *Alice's Adventures in Wonderland* and *Through the Looking Glass*, the amusing and strange journeys of a little girl named Alice. *The Jungle Books*, by Rudyard Kipling, introduced Mowgli, the boy who was raised by a wolf. Robert Louis Stevenson wrote the exciting tale of *Treasure Island*. George MacDonald created *At the Back of the North Wind*, a magical, mysterious tale of wonder. Louisa May Alcott's *Little Women*, the story of a New England family during the Civil war, was an instant success. Frances Hodgson Burnett wrote *Little Lord Fauntleroy*, a story about an American boy from a poor family who suddenly finds himself the heir to an English earldom. *The Adventures of Tom Sawyer* and *Huckleberry Finn*, in which two boys have many adventures, are as much fun to

read today as when Mark Twain wrote them more than 100 years ago.

Best-Loved Books of the 1900's *Wind in the Willows*, by Kenneth Grahame introduced to young readers a whole new cast of delightful riverbank and field creatures. E. B. White wrote *Charlotte's Web*, in which a spider teaches about love, and *The Trumpet of the Swan*, the remarkable achievements of an ambitious trumpeter swan. J. R. R. Tolkien's *The Hobbit* and "Ring" stories are marvelous tales of gold, a magic ring, dragons, trolls, and elves. The "Doctor Dolittle" books, by Hugh Lofting, tell of the plump doctor who was able to talk to animals, including the fabulous "Pushmi-Pullyu." C. S. Lewis's "Narnia" books are the adventures of four children in the magic land of Narnia. P. L. Travers created *Mary Poppins*, a most wonderful governess with amazing talents. And A. A. Milne's "Pooh" stories featured the endearing, slow-witted toy bear Winnie-the-Pooh, his stuffed animal friends, and the little boy Christopher Robin.

Magazines and Comic Books The first edition of the famous children's magazine *St. Nicholas*, was published in 1873. Louisa May Alcott, Rudyard Kipling, Frances Hodgson Burnett, and Mark Twain were only a few of the great authors who entertained children in this wonderful magazine, which helped to make children's literature more creative and original. Many magazines just for children have been published since that time. *Jack and Jill*, *Highlights for Children*, *Cricket*, and *Humpty Dumpty's Magazine* are four current favorites.

Comic books are read by almost all American children, and many others, too, although parents do not always approve of them. They have been published in the United States since 1911. These brightly colored but often crudely drawn "picture maga-

◀ A scene from The Yearling, *by Marjorie Kinnan Rawlings. The story is about a lonely boy who makes friends with a young deer. This illustration is by N.C. Wyeth.*

zines" are packed with adventure and excitement and are easy and fun to read. Some comics are educational. They offer stories from the Bible, history, the lives of great people, and current events.

Picture Books and Illustrations
The drawings and paintings that illustrate children's books are sometimes more important than the words. These illustrations are a very special form of art. Several of the great illustrators (book artists) of the past were Kate Greenaway, Beatrix Potter (who wrote the Peter Rabbit books), and Randolph Caldecott. The Caldecott Award is given every year in the United States for the best illustrated children's book. George Cruikshank illustrated the books of Charles Dickens and *Grimm's Fairy Tales*. Sir John Tenniel won fame as the illustrator of *Alice's Adventures in Wonderland*. Arthur Rackham painted the pictures for Sir James Barrie's *Peter Pan*, the story of Never-Never Land and the little boy who would not grow up. Ernest H. Shepard was the name of the man who drew Winnie-the-Pooh. The humorous drawings of Maurice Sendak delight children in his own books, *Where the Wild Things Are*, *In the Night Kitchen*, and others.

Poetry and Tales of Other Lands
Much poetry has wonderful sound and rhythm. *A Child's Garden of Verses*, by Robert Louis Stevenson, and *Songs for Childhood*, by Walter de la Mare, are two collections that are delightful to read out loud. *The Night Before Christmas*, by Clement C. Moore, is one the best-loved poems ever written. Theodore Seuss Geisel ("Dr. Seuss") writes funny rhyme-stories, such as *The Cat in the Hat*.

Ballads are another form of poetry. They tell a story in verse. Early ballads were sung, often by wandering minstrels. One of the most famous of all the heroes in ballads is Robin

Before 1800 the few books that were written specially for children tried to teach good behavior or school subjects. But during the 1800's children's literature came into its own. These were the years of the Grimm brothers, Hans Christian Andersen, Lewis Carroll, Louisa May Alcott, Anna Sewell, Robert Louis Stevenson, Jules Verne, and many other famous writers. Can you think of one book or story written by each of them?

TERMS USED IN LITERATURE

Character
A person or animal in a story.

Fiction
A made-up story, usually meant to entertain.

Nonfiction
Reading for information, made up of facts.

Fantasy
A make-believe story, often with strange, nonreal characters such as fairies or monsters.

Career Story
A story telling about a particular kind of job or profession, such as that of a doctor, dancer, pilot, or actor.

Folk Tale
A story or legend passed on from generation to generation.

Classic
A book or poem that has won literary fame; one that will last because it is considered by many people to be very good.

Mystery
A story about a puzzling crime or secret.

The first children's "encyclopedia" was written about 1075 by Anselm, Archbishop of Canterbury, England. It was in Latin and, of course, had to be laboriously copied by monks; so very few children must have read it!

Hood, the English outlaw who was a friend to poor and oppressed people. Ballads describing Robin Hood's struggles against the Sheriff of Nottingham were first sung in the 1500's. Heroes of American ballads much loved by children include Casey Jones, the railroad engineer, and Jesse James, the outlaw.

Stories about other lands and customs have always intrigued children. Every country in the world has its own special folk tales. Rudyard Kipling's *Just So Stories*, which tell "how the camel got his hump" and "how the elephant got his trunk," are based on the folklore of India.

Fascinating tales are told in Europe, South America, Africa, the Orient, and in the legends of American Indians. Books have been made collecting all these stories. *Hans Brinker, or, the Silver Skates*, by Mary Mapes Dodge, is a story about Holland. *Pinocchio*, the story of a puppet who wanted to become a real boy, is by the Italian writer known as Collodi. Johanna Spyri's *Heidi* is the joyful story of a Swiss girl and her grandfather. These stories and many others have been translated into many languages and have delighted children everywhere for many years.

What's Happening Today The American Booksellers Association started *Children's Book Week* in 1919. All over the United States, one special week each year is devoted to children's books. Libraries have children's departments and special librarians. Bookstores often have huge sections of children's books. Encyclopedias for children have been published since 1910. Some publishing companies publish only children's books.

Today, more and more writers and illustrators are creating children's books that deal with modern life and its problems. There are books about drugs, death, adoption, divorce, prejudice, the environment, urban prob-

▲ *A modern illustration for a story from* Tales From Uncle Remus, *by Joel Chandler Harris.*

lems, and women's liberation. Irene Hunt's *Up a Road Slowly* treats realistically the problems of growing up. Also included among the best children's literature written today are Scott O'Dell's *Island of the Blue Dolphins*, Madeleine L'Engle's *A Wrinkle in Time*, and *A Ring of Endless Light*, William Armstrong's *Sounder*, and Katherine Paterson's *Bridge to Terabithia*, and *Jacob I Have Loved*. You may enjoy reading all of these and many others. They will be a part of you as long as you live.

For further information on:

Authors, *see* AESOP; ALCOTT, LOUISA MAY; ANDERSEN, HANS CHRISTIAN; BARRIE, JAMES M.; BAUM, L. FRANK; BLUME, JUDY; BURNETT, FRANCES HODGSON; CARROLL, LEWIS; GRAHAME, KENNETH; GRIMM BROTHERS; HARRIS, JOEL CHANDLER; IRVING, WASHINGTON; KIPLING, RUDYARD; LA FONTAINE, JEAN DE; LEAR, EDWARD; MILNE, A. A.; PERRAULT, CHARLES; POTTER, BEATRIX; RILEY, JAMES WHITCOMB; SPYRI, JOHANNA; TWAIN, MARK; WIGGIN, KATE DOUGLAS; WILDER, LAURA INGALLS.

Awards, *see* CALDECOTT AWARD, NEWBERY MEDAL.

How Literature Gets into Print, *see* BOOK, COMMERCIAL ART, PRINTING, PUBLISHING.

Kinds of Literature, *see* AUTOBIOGRAPHY, BIOGRAPHY, FABLE, FAIRY TALE, LIMERICK, NOVEL, NURSERY RHYMES, POETRY, SHORT STORY.

CHILE Chile is a narrow ribbon of land in South America between the Andes Mountains and the Pacific Ocean. It is more than 2,600 miles (4,180 km) long but only about 100 miles (160 km) wide in most places. (See the map with the article on SOUTH AMERICA.)

Chile has almost every kind of climate and landscape. The Andes Mountains—some of the world's highest mountains—rise along its backbone. Skiers come to this area of glaciers, volcanoes, alpine lakes, and dense forests. The Atacama Desert, in northern Chile, is one of the driest deserts on Earth. The region has few people, but the country's most valuable natural resources are found there—huge deposits of copper, nitrates, borax, and sulfur.

Most Chileans live on farms in the warm, rainy central valley. Large crops of grapes, citrus fruits, potatoes, olives, and grains are grown on the fertile farms. The capital city, Santiago, is a large manufacturing center. Other important cities are Valparaiso, the principal port, and Concepción, center of the steel industry. Chile is one of South America's leading industrial nations.

Chile ends at Cape Horn, south of Tierra del Fuego. This large island's name means "Land of Fire." The land near the Cape is rainy, cold, and windy. Until the Panama Canal was built, ships had to struggle through

▲ *Ice formation in the waters around Tierra del Fuego (Land of Fire), a group of islands off southern Chile. There are many glaciers in this area.*

Chile is so narrow that no Chilean lives more than 250 miles (400 km) from the sea. It is the longest country (north to south) in the world.

CHILE

Capital City: Santiago (4,800,000 people).
Area: 295,732 square miles (765,945 sq. km).
Population: 12,866,000.
Government: Republic.
Natural Resources: Copper, borax, sulfur, nitrate, iron ore, coal, and other minerals.
Export Products: Copper, paper and pulp, lumber, nitrate.
Unit of Money: New Peso.
Official Language: Spanish.

▲ *The Atacama Desert, which lies in northern Chile, is the driest place on Earth.*

the Straits of Magellan north of Tierra del Fuego or battle the fierce winds by "rounding the Horn."

Nearly two-thirds of Chilean people are *mestizos*, or mixed Spanish and Indian, although some are full-blooded Indians. Almost all the people speak Spanish. Nearly 90 percent of all Chileans can read and write.

The northern part of Chile was part of the fabulous Inca empire. The southern part was inhabited by Araucanian Indians. Chile was conquered by Pedro de Valdivia for Spain in 1540. Valdivia founded Santiago, later to be Chile's capital, in 1541. Spanish colonists made fortunes raising cattle and wheat, using Indians, and later black slaves, for labor. Chile won independence from Spain in 1818, with the help of José San Martin, an Argentine general, and Bernardo O'Higgins, a Chilean patriot. O'Higgins wrote Chile's first constitution. He was forced to resign in 1823 after his attempts to control the power of the country's wealthy landowners.

Chile has had dictatorial and democratic governments. In 1973, military leaders overthrew the government. In 1989, General Pinochet's military goverment was defeated in free presidential elections.

ALSO READ: SOUTH AMERICA.

CHINA

Capital City: Peking (Beijing, 5,900,000 people).

Area: 3,705,390 square miles (9,596,961 sq. km).

Population: 1,070,000,000.

Government: People's Republic.

Natural Resources: Coal, oil and natural gas, iron ore, gold, tin, tungsten.

Export Products: Oil and oil products, textiles, chemicals, various other manufactures.

Unit of Money: Yuan.

Official Language: Chinese.

CHINA China is about the same size as the United States, but it has the largest population of any nation in the world. About 22 out of every 100 persons on Earth live in China.

Whenever you read about China you may find the same Chinese names spelled in different ways. This is because Chinese is not written in the Roman alphabet, but in characters. Scholars have devised ways of writing Chinese names in our alphabet. One method, the Wade-Giles system, was developed in the 1800's. But since 1979, the Chinese government has used another system, called Pinyin. As a result, many familiar spellings have been changed. For example, China's leader from 1949 to 1976 was called Mao Tse-tung in the Wade-Giles system. In the Pinyin system, he was now named Mao Zedong. This article uses the older spellings familiar to Westerners. The Pinyin spellings are in parentheses.

China stretches from the deserts and mountains of Central Asia to the Pacific Ocean. Many climates and kinds of land—cold high mountains, fertile subtropical valleys, and burning deserts—are found in this vast country. China's fertile land is located in a basin surrounded by mountains and desert. The plains and gentle hills of the north, west, and southwest are along the coast. Two great rivers, the Yellow (Huang He) and the Yangtze (Yangzi Jiang) begin in the mountains of western China and flow into the Pacific. More than half of all the Chinese people are jammed into these two river valleys. Indeed, most Chinese live in the eastern and southeastern third of the country. (See the map in the article ASIA.)

China has several extremely large cities. But about 78 out of every 100 people still live in country areas. China is mainly a farming country. Farming employs 69 out of every 100 workers. Grain is the leading food. Rice is the main crop in the warmer

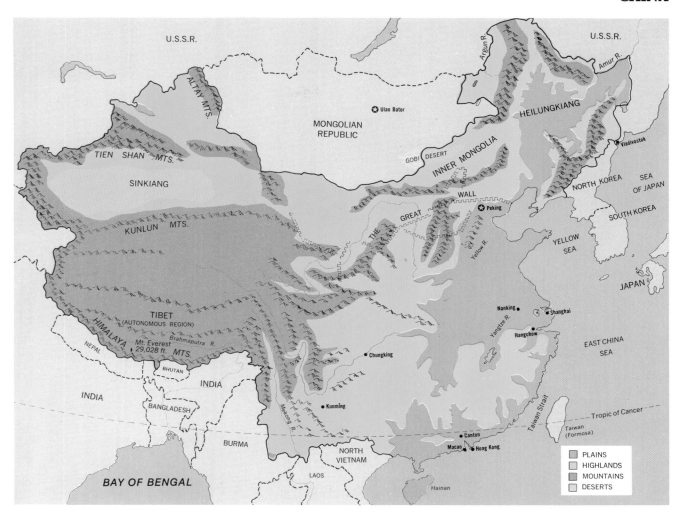

south and wheat is the main crop in the cooler north. Corn, sorghum, and millet are also popular, especially in the north. Cotton, potatoes, soybeans, tobacco, tea, fruits, livestock, and vegetables are other major products. Fish, shellfish, and seaweed are popular foods in some areas. Meat makes up only a small part of people's diets, though most people enjoy pork on special occasions. Few Chinese eat butter and cheese.

China has great wealth in natural resources and is gradually becoming an industrial country. It has also become a nuclear power. China's huge population (over one billion), which increases by about 14 million persons a year, is a major problem that hinders modern development.

The family has always been at the center of Chinese life. People feel that

their first duty is to their family. Much of this belief comes from Confucianism, which also teaches respect and obedience to elders, loyalty to rulers and social harmony.

The Communist government of China has tried to convince the people that their first duty is to the country. But family life is still very important. The Communists have made other changes. For example, rich landowners and factory workers have had to give their property to the state.

China's written history goes back over 3,000 years. The Chinese were the first to develop gunpowder, paper, porcelain, printing, and silk. Neighboring nations such as Korea, Japan, and Vietnam have borrowed from China's science, art, writing system, literature, religion, and methods of government.

▲ The Chinese are part of the Mongoloid racial group, which is characterized by dark, straight hair and high cheekbones. A small fold of skin on the upper eyelid gives their eyes an almond shape.

537

CHINESE HISTORY AT A GLANCE

5000 B.C. Village farming communities along Yellow River
1500 Shang dynasty begins first historical period in China
1027 Chou dynasty founded
551 Birth of Confucius
221–207 Ch'in dynasty unites China
214 Building of the Great Wall
202–A.D.9 Han dynasty
A.D. 220–264 China divided into three kingdoms
618 Tang dynasty founded
932 Wood block printing adopted
960–1275 Sung dynasty
976–997 T'ai Tsung completes reunion of China
1000 Invention of gunpowder
1120 Chinese invent playing cards
1210 Mongols invade China
1468 Ming dynasty founded
1556 Over 800,000 die in earthquake in Shensi, Shansi, and Honan provinces
1644–1912 Manchu dynasty
1839–42 First Opium War
1900 Boxer Rebellion
1924 Sun Yatsen establishes Chinese republican government
1927 Civil war in China
1934 Mao Tse-tung leads Communists on Long March
1937 Japan invades China
1949 Communists declare People's Republic
1966 "Cultural Revolution" in China
1976 Death of Mao Tse-tung

▲ *A pottery soldier found buried by the tomb of the emperor Shih-Huangdi, who ruled in the 200's* B.C.

The Great Wall of China. On the righthand side, peasant workers excavate the earth and ram it into place using wooden frames. On the left, a completed section of wall, with its battlements and paved roadway, leads to a fortified watchtower.

jade burial suit made for
Liu Sheng, who died
100's B.C. It contained
carefully shaped pieces
...le.

philosopher Confucius
born in 551 B.C. The
of his works later
...me the focus of learning in
...a.

...he emperor Han Kuang-
...who ruled in the 1st
...ry A.D. The emperors
...surrounded by attendants
...servants and lived lives of
...luxury.

◄ Tz'u Hsi, Empress-
Dowager of China until 1908,
was firmly opposed to foreign
influence in China.

▲ Mao Tse-tung, the Chinese
Communist leader, who
proclaimed a People's
Republic in 1949 after a bitter
civil war.

◄ A Japanese painting of a
battle during the war with
China in 1894.

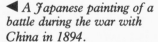

▲ *People in China have always been very fond of gardens. Often they had lakes and little pagodas, like this modern garden.*

▼ *Everyone works together to make new farmland in China. Despite progress in the cities, 78 out of every 100 people still live in the country.*

China had little contact with the Western world for hundreds of years. In the 1800's, Europeans, led by the British, tried to open China to trade and other relations. It was a time when China was weak. In the end the Western powers, including the United States, established political and trade relations with China. This happened in 1901 after the Boxer Rebellion in which Chinese terrorists tried to get rid of all foreigners.

Dr. Sun Yatsen led a revolution in 1912 that overthrew the last dynasty (ruling family). China became a republic but was torn by international upheaval. After the death of Sun Yatsen in 1925, the competition between the Nationalists and the Communists for the control of China began. After 1937, however, the Nationalists and Communists joined forces to beat back the Japanese invasion of China. Japan's surrender in 1945 touched off a civil war between the Communists under Mao Tse-tung (Mao Zedong) and the Nationalists under Chiang Kai-shek (Jiang Jieshi). By 1949 the Communists had conquered mainland China and driven the Nationalist government to the island of Taiwan. The Communists proclaimed the People's Republic of China on the mainland, with Mao as chairman.

In 1971, Communist China re-

▲ *The "Forbidden City" was once the royal part of Peking, where ordinary people could not go. Today its palaces serve as museums for Chinese works of art.*

placed Nationalist China (Taiwan) in the United Nations. Since then, Communist China has become an important world power, having diplomatic and trade relations with many Western nations.

Changes occurred rapidly within the country after the death of Mao in 1976. The new leaders set about modernizing China's economy. While Mao had worked to develop farming and the countryside, the new leaders, such as Teng Hsiao-p'ing (Deng Xiaoping), helped industries to develop in the cities and towns. They also gave farmers more control over their land and encouraged the building of factories in country areas, so that peasants can leave farming and become factory workers.

But the old communism still prevails. In 1989, the Chinese People's Army shot and killed 2,600 students and workers demonstrating for greater freedom in Beijing.

ALSO READ: ANCIENT CIVILIZATIONS; ASIA; CHIANG KAI-SHEK; CHINESE; CHOU EN-LAI; COMMUNISM; GOBI DESERT; GREAT WALL OF CHINA; MAO TSE-TUNG; MONGOLIA; ORIENTAL ART; PEKING; POLO, MARCO; SHANGHAI; SUN YAT-SEN; TAIWAN; TENG HSIAO-P'ING; YANGTZE RIVER; YELLOW RIVER.

CHINA, NATIONALIST
see TAIWAN.

CHINESE Chinese is very different from English and from most other major languages. For one thing, the language is spoken in hundreds of different ways (*dialects*). A person from one area often cannot understand a person from another area. The two most important dialects are Cantonese and Mandarin. Most Chinese people living in the United States speak Cantonese, a southern dialect. Mandarin, a dialect of northern China, is spoken by more Chinese than any other dialect.

People often say that the Chinese "sing" their language. Chinese has a singsong quality because most words are only one syllable long and because words have more than one meaning—the speaker's tone of voice gives the specific meaning of the word. For example, the word *ma* means "mother," "huh?" or "horse," depending on the tone of voice. The four tones of Chinese are high, rising, falling, and low. To get an idea of what this is like, try saying the name "John" as though you were calling John to lunch. Now say "John" as though you are angry with him. Hear the difference?

But the most fascinating thing about Chinese is its writing. It has no alphabet, no ABC's. Instead, signs called *characters* are used, one for each spoken word. Originally, characters were drawings of the things they represented. A circle with a dot at its center meant "sun," and a stick figure meant "man." The characters were simplified over the years, and most no longer look like the things they stand for.

Westerners have thought of several ways to write Chinese with the Roman alphabet. The Communist Chinese have also adopted a system for doing this, called Pinyin, which means "phonetic script" in Chinese. The Roman alphabet is used in Pinyin, except "v," because Chinese has no "vee" sound. Three sounds are added—SH, CH, and ZH. The four tones are shown by marks—a bar (ˉ) for high, an acute accent (ˊ) for rising, a grave accent (ˋ) for falling, and a circumflex (ˆ) for low.

A new girl going to a school for the first time would say to her new classmates, "Zâo. Wó xíng Chīn." (ZHOW. WUH SHING CHIN.) "Good morning. My name is Chin."

ALSO READ: ALPHABET, CHINA, LANGUAGES, HIEROGLYPHICS, WRITTEN LANGUAGE.

CHINOOK INDIANS The Chinook Indians lived near the mouth of the Columbia River in an area that now lies in the states of Washington and Oregon. They were skilled sailors whose dugout canoes roamed as far north along the Pacific Coast as Vancouver Island.

Once a year, when the salmon ran, all the Chinook left their villages and went salmon fishing. They caught salmon, roasted the fish, and ate as much as they wanted for ten days. They then sold or bartered smoked salmon for goods from other Indians. The Chinook also bought furs from other tribes and traded them for blankets and kettles brought by white traders on sailing ships. They traveled so widely that a simple version of their complex language, called Chinook jargon, became the common language for trade and business in the Pacific Northwest.

Only a few survivors remain from the Chinook tribe of traders and fishermen. Most of the tribe died in an epidemic of malaria in 1829. Those who were left joined the Chehalis Indians who took over Chinook territory.

ALSO READ: INDIANS, AMERICAN.

▲ *An example of Chinese writing. The characters are drawn with a brush rather than a pen.*

If all the people in China stood on each other's shoulders they would make a chain three times longer than the distance between the Earth and the moon.

More than 1,400,000 tons of cocoa beans are produced each year to make chocolate products. The Swiss are at the top of the world's chocolate-eating ladder. They eat 22 pounds (10 kg) per person every year.

CHIPPENDALE, THOMAS see FURNITURE.

CHIPPEWA INDIANS see OJIBWA INDIANS.

CHIROPRACTIC Chiropractic is a system of treating illnesses or injuries that is based on the theory that the nervous system controls the normal functioning of our bodies. Any pressure or tension on the spinal column or nerves may, therefore, cause disease or interfere with its cure.

The principles of chiropractic were set out by Daniel D. Palmer of Davenport, Iowa in 1895. Chiropractors believe that the vertebrae (the bones of the spine) can cause illness by moving out of place and pressing on veins, arteries, or nerves. Treatment usually involves manipulation or massage of the spine.

Another related system of treatment is *osteopathy*, invented in 1874 by Andrew T. Still. Both systems are now practiced in many parts of the world, though they are not fully recognized by the medical profession. In many cases of back pain or other spine-related disorders manipulation does bring relief to the patient.

CHIVALRY see KNIGHTHOOD.

CHLOROPHYLL see PHOTOSYNTHESIS.

CHOCOLATE What is the Western world's most popular flavor for candy, bakery products, ice cream, and beverages? If you say "Chocolate," you are right. It has nutritional value because it contains fat, carbohydrate, and protein. When mixed with sugar to make candy, it provides a good source of quick energy. Europeans did not know about chocolate until the Spanish explorers met the Aztec and Mayan Indians of Mexico in the early 1500's. During the next 200 years, people all over Europe became fond of chocolate.

Chocolate comes from oval-shaped *cacao beans*. These beans are found in pods that grow on cacao trees. After the beans are removed from the pods, they are allowed to ferment and dry. The cacao beans are roasted, then shelled, and ground into small pieces. The grinding releases *cocoa butter*, an oily substance, from the seeds. Cocoa butter is combined with pieces of the beans to make *chocolate liquor*. Chocolate liquor is the base of all chocolate products. It is cooled and hardened into blocks to make baker's or unsweetened chocolate. Sugar is added to it to make sweet and semisweet chocolate. When sugar and milk are added, milk chocolate results. *Cocoa powder*, made from the chocolate liquor, is used to make a tasty, hot drink.

Although "white" chocolate tastes like chocolate, it contains no cocoa solids and cannot technically be called chocolate. It is a blend of vegetable fat, sugar, dry milk solids, vanilla and cocoa butter. The butter creates a chocolate fragrance. Milk and vanilla provide the flavor.

ALSO READ: CANDY, NUTRITION.

CHOCTAW INDIANS Like most American Indian tribes that lived in the southeastern United States, the Choctaws were excellent farmers. Corn was their principal crop. They weeded and cultivated their fields with wooden hoes and planting sticks. They made utensils, such as ladles, from gourds. They collected wild fruits, berries, and roots, caught fish, and hunted with bows and arrows. They built homes out of a framework of poles covered with woven willow, bark, reeds, or plaster.

▲ *Chocolate comes from the beans that develop in the large pods of the cacao tree. Cocoa, another form of chocolate, was drunk by the Aztecs of Central America even before Europeans arrived.*

They made clothes from animal skins, woven grasses, or bark.

Explorers and fellow Indians gave the Choctaws the nickname of "Flatheads." The Choctaws and several other tribes put a flat board on a baby's head while the skull bones were still soft. As the baby grew, the top of his or her head would flatten.

Choctaws played a rough game much like today's lacrosse. All the young men of a village took part in the game.

The Choctaws were moved from their lands in Mississippi and Alabama to Indian Territory (now Oklahoma) in the early 1800's. They adopted many customs of the American settlers and became known as one of the "Five Civilized Tribes." The others are Cherokees, Chickasaws, Creeks, and Seminoles.

ALSO READ: INDIANS, AMERICAN; LACROSSE.

CHOPIN, FRÉDÉRIC FRANÇOIS (1810–1849)

The great Polish pianist and composer, Frédéric Chopin, wrote many beautiful pieces of music for the piano. He has been called "the poet of the piano."

Frédéric Chopin was born near Warsaw, Poland. Music fascinated him at a very early age. At age seven he began to write piano pieces. He first played the piano in a concert on his eighth birthday.

In 1830 Chopin was in Austria when he learned that the Russians had captured Warsaw. He never returned to Poland, but his spirit remained there. Some of Chopin's pieces were stirring calls for Polish independence. He settled in Paris, and leading poets, artists, and musicians living there became his friends.

Chopin gave public concerts, taught piano students, and composed. Some of his *nocturnes* (compositions for the piano) have lovely, flowing, and restful melodies. They are among the best nocturnes ever composed. Polish nobles of that time danced the *polonaise*, and the peasants danced the lively *mazurka*. Chopin, remembering his homeland, wrote music for both dances. He also wrote two concertos for piano and orchestra, as well as works for the piano alone. His use of harmony and rhythm influenced composers such as Richard Wagner, Franz Liszt, and Claude Debussy.

Although Chopin fell in love with several women, he never married. He was unwell for most of his life and died of tuberculosis at age 39.

ALSO READ: COMPOSER; DEBUSSY, CLAUDE; LISZT, FRANZ; MUSIC; PIANO; WAGNER, RICHARD.

CHOPSTICKS

The Chinese have used chopsticks for about 2,500 years, and call them *kwai-tze*, or the "quick ones." These all-purpose cooking and eating utensils can be made of bone, ivory, wood, metal, or plastic. They are also used by the Japanese, Koreans, and Indochinese.

Chopsticks are held in one hand. The top of the lower stick rests in the groove at the base of the thumb. The lower part of the stick rests on the ring finger. It does not move. The second stick is held by the thumb and index and middle fingers. This stick moves, pinching the small pieces of food against the first stick. Get a pair of chopsticks (most Chinese restaurants will give them to you) and practice. Soon you will be able to scoop up even the most slippery foods, such as rice and scrambled eggs.

ALSO READ: KNIVES, FORKS, AND SPOONS.

CHORAL MUSIC

Music sung by a *choir*, or group of singers, is known as choral music. Religious choral music may be sung in churches. Non-

▲ *A Choctaw Indian employed by a lumber company in the forests of southeastern Oklahoma. Many Choctaws now work in the lumber industry.*

▲ *Frédéric Chopin, Polish composer of romantic music.*

▲ *A part of a piece of choral music for mixed voices by Samuel Barber. The first four lines of music are for the four types of voices: soprano (the highest voice of females and young boys), alto (a low female voice), tenor (the highest man's voice), bass (the lowest man's voice). The two bottom lines of music are for the piano.*

▼ *Much choral music is performed in churches. Here, the choir sits in special stalls.*

religious choral music may form part of long works such as operas. Short choral works may be sung by groups of singers in choral societies, or glee clubs. Sometimes all the members of the choir follow the same tune, or part; at other times the choir may be divided into as many as eight different groups, each singing a different tune at the same time.

The ancient Hebrews worshiped God with choral singing. Groups of singers in the early Christian churches sang words from the Bible. They all sang the same part. This is called *plainsong* or *Gregorian chant*, which is still used in some music.

Choral music with more than one part became popular in Europe after the 900's. Such music is called *polyphonic* music. It was written both as church and nonreligious (*secular*) music well into the 1600's. Two important song forms were the *madrigal* and the *motet*.

After 1600, composers began to write musical works known as cantatas and oratorios. Choral music played a large part in these. A *cantata* is usually short. It contains solos, or arias (for one singer), duets (for two singers), and choral music. Some of the most famous religious cantatas were written by the German composer Johann Sebastian Bach. Many nonreligious cantatas were also writ-

ten. Bach himself wrote a humorous one called the "Coffee Cantata." An *oratorio* is a longer work, usually on a religious subject. Choral music is the most important part of an oratorio. The composer George Frederick Handel brought this type of work to its peak with his *Messiah*, first performed in 1742.

One of the greatest works of the German composer Ludwig van Beethoven is the *Ninth Symphony*, also known as the "Choral Symphony." It was composed in the early 1800's. A choir and soloists join the orchestra in the magnificent final section.

Very large choirs were used for choral music in the 1800's and the early 1900's. Bach's great religious work, the *St. Matthew Passion*, was performed in 1829 by a chorus of 300. Choirs at some festivals have contained as many as 3,000 singers.

Many very fine choral works have been written in the 1900's. Two of the most famous modern composers of choral music were the Russian-American Igor Stravinsky and Benjamin Britten, an Englishman.

ALSO READ: BACH FAMILY; BEETHOVEN, LUDWIG VAN; CHORUSES AND CHOIRS; HANDEL, GEORGE FREDERICK; MUSIC; OPERA; STRAVINSKY, IGOR.

CHOREOGRAPHY see DANCE.

CHORUSES AND CHOIRS

Two kinds of singing groups—choruses and choirs—are very nearly the same. These two words are sometimes used for exactly the same thing. Choir usually refers to the singing group of a church. A chorus is most often nonreligious, such as a school chorus, concert group, or the chorus of an opera company.

The singing group may be of mixed voices whether it is a chorus or a choir. The women sing soprano and alto parts, and the men sing tenor and bass. They sometimes sing in *unison*, all on the same note. Women in a mixed choir are usually placed in front of the men, with the sopranos on the right side of the stage in front of the tenors and the altos on the left in front of the basses.

Some choirs are made up of all men, or men and boys. If there are boys, they sing the parts taken by women in a mixed chorus. There are also choruses of all women. Boys and girls may make up a junior choir in church. Singers in a boys' choir are often called *choristers*. Choral groups in school may be called *glee clubs*.

Music for choral groups may be written with a musical accompaniment. If the group sings without accompaniment, it is said to sing *a cappella*, an Italian phrase that means "in the manner of the chapel."

Many kinds of music have been written for choral singers—religious anthems, cantatas, oratorios, music written for concert performance, *arrangements* (rewritten from another kind of music) of Negro spirituals, folk songs, and Christmas carols.

Some of the best-known choral groups are the Vienna Boys' Choir; the Mormon Tabernacle Choir of Salt Lake City, Utah; the Bach Festival Choir of Bethlehem, Pennsylvania; the Westminster Choir of Princeton, New Jersey; the Robert Shaw Chorale; and the Don Cossack singers.

ALSO READ: CHORAL MUSIC, OPERA, SINGING.

CHOU EN-LAI (1898–1976) Chou

En-lai was one of the leaders of modern China. He was born in Kiangsu Province in the eastern part of China. As a young man he not only had a classical Chinese education, but also studied at a college run by American missionaries in the city of Tientsin. He later traveled to France and Ger-

many to do further study.

Chou En-lai returned home in 1926. China, in those days, was torn by internal struggles. He joined forces in 1931 with Mao Tse-tung, a leader in the Chinese Communist party, and became a political leader in one of the main Communist armies. Chiang Kai-shek, who opposed Communism, sought to destroy the Communist movement and eventually drove them into a rural base in southeastern China. Further attacks by Chiang Kai-shek and his armies forced them to seek—by what has come to be known as "The Long March"—another base in Yenan in northern China. From this base, the Communists fought both the Nationalist Army and the Japanese.

When the Communists gained control in 1949, Chou became premier and foreign minister of the People's Republic of China. At the Bandung Conference in 1955, he helped forge economic cooperation among many Asian and African nations. In 1972, Chou met several times with U.S. President Richard Nixon. Chou was largely responsible for establishing friendly relations between Communist China and the West.

ALSO READ: CHIANG KAI-SHEK, CHINA, COMMUNISM, MAO TSE-TUNG.

▲ *Large choral works often require a great number of performers. Here, a chorus and an orchestra are recording a major work.*

▲ *Chou En-lai, a former leader of Communist China.*

▲ *A jeweled cross, symbol of Christianity, from Burgos, in Spain. Christianity spread quickly after the A.D. 300's.*

CHRISTIANITY One of the great religions of the world is Christianity. It is based on the teachings of Jesus Christ. Jesus lived almost 2,000 years ago in the ancient country of Palestine (now part of Jordan and Israel) on the eastern shores of the Mediterranean Sea. He lived a life of poverty and humility, traveling on foot and preaching to the people. Jesus taught that men should love God and one another. Many people began to believe his teachings, but others misunderstood him. Jesus was a Jew, and some Jewish religious leaders in Palestine resented his challenge of their leadership. The Romans, who ruled Palestine at the time, saw him as a serious troublemaker. Jesus was sentenced to die by being nailed to a cross.

From his followers, Jesus had chosen twelve men to be his Apostles, to help him teach. According to them, Jesus appeared again, alive, three days after his death. He then stayed on earth for 40 days before going bodily to heaven. Most of the Apostles then set out bravely to spread the teachings of Jesus. The most famous of the Apostles were Saint Peter and Saint Paul, who founded many of the first Christian churches. Their stories of the life of Jesus are written down in the New Testament of the Bible.

Christianity Grows and Divides The belief of Christianity spread rapidly through the lands of the Roman Empire, but the early Christians faced terrible persecution.

Some were thrown into the Roman sports arena to be eaten by lions because they were teaching a strange, new religion opposed to the idea that the Roman emperors were gods themselves. Others were burned to death. In 313, the Roman Emperor Constantine ordered that Christians were to be allowed to worship freely. This was known as the Edict of Milan. During the following centuries, Christianity spread throughout Europe.

The Roman Empire collapsed in the late 400's, and the people of Europe fought among themselves for the next 500 years. They forgot most of the things that the Romans had taught them. During this time, a few holy men called *monks* devoted their lives to the study and spread of Christianity. They helped to keep the religion alive by preserving its sacred writings and beliefs. These monks often were the only people at the time who could read and write.

By the 800's, Christians had begun to disagree about many religious and political matters, and they split into two large groups in 1054. One group became known as the Western or Roman Catholic Church, whose members claimed that the pope in Rome was the religious leader. The other group was the Eastern Orthodox church, whose members believed that the patriarch in Constantinople (now Istanbul) was the only true head of all Christians. The 1500's brought another split. Some Roman Catholics did not agree with the practices of the Church. The German priest, Martin Luther, led the way. At first he wanted to correct abuses of authority in the Church. Later, he disagreed with church belief and denied the authority of the pope. Other leaders in various parts of Europe began reform groups and new churches. The split in the Church widened and could not be bridged. This split is known as the *Protestant Reformation.*

Christianity was now divided into

▼ *St. Paul was one of Jesus' Apostles. He traveled widely, founding many of the first Christian churches. This map shows the routes he followed.*

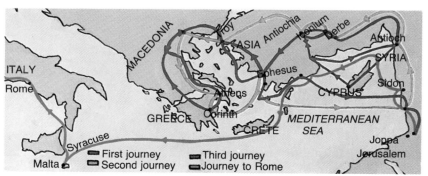

various parts—the Roman Catholic Church, the Eastern Orthodox groups, and many Protestant sects. Church leaders in this century have made progress in bringing the main Christian church groups closer together. These efforts are called *ecumenical movements*. Today, almost one billion people are Christians. Christianity has more followers than any other religion in the world. Christians practice their faith in many different ways, but most share the belief in Jesus as the Son of God and the Savior of mankind.

ALSO READ: APOSTLES; BIBLE; JESUS CHRIST; LUTHER, MARTIN; ORTHODOX CHURCH; PAUL, SAINT; PROTESTANT CHURCHES; PROTESTANT REFORMATION; ROMAN CATHOLIC CHURCH; ROME, ANCIENT.

CHRISTIAN SCIENCE Mary Baker Eddy founded the Christian Science religion in Boston, Massachusetts, in 1879. Today the "Mother Church" is The First Church of Christ, Scientist, in Boston. There are over 3,000 Christian Science churches and societies throughout the world, most of them in the United States.

Mary Baker Eddy explained her beliefs in her book *Science and Health with Key to the Scriptures*, published in 1875. Basically, it teaches that God is the source of all that is good and of nothing else. Only good is real and lasting. Whatever is not good, such as illness, sin, suffering, and death, comes from misunderstanding God. Evil is to be conquered by learning to know and express God as Jesus Christ did. Christian Scientists believe that through prayer and studying the Bible, the power to heal can be demonstrated today as in New Testament days.

Church services are led by church members elected as *readers*. Qualified members who devote their full time to healing are called *practitioners*.

There are Christian Science reading rooms in many cities, where people may read publications of the church. *The Christian Science Monitor*, a world-renowned daily newspaper, is published in Boston.

ALSO READ: CHRISTIANITY.

CHRISTMAS This day was set to celebrate the birthday of Jesus Christ. For many children in the United States, Christmas is trees with glittering ornaments, holiday cookies, a turkey dinner, the sound of carols, and Santa Claus. Christians in other lands celebrate in ways special to them.

It is not known exactly when Christ was born, so most Christians celebrate it on December 25. The Christmas story in the Bible tells of shepherds watching their flocks one night. An angel appeared and told the shepherds that a Savior had been born in Bethlehem, and that they should go to see him. Later, the Three Wise Men, or Kings, brought gifts of gold, frankincense, and myrrh to the Christ Child.

Many legends and customs surround the Christmas celebration. Among them is the favorite tale of Saint Nicholas, whose bulging bag overflows with gifts for "good" children. The original Saint Nicholas was a bishop who lived in what is now Turkey about 1,700 years ago. He spent his life doing good deeds. The Dutch people called him *Sinterklaas*. His fame spread to America, where his name was changed to *Santa Claus*. Today Americans think of him as that plump, jolly fellow who travels in a reindeer-drawn sled. The children of Italy have the good fairy La Belfana in place of Santa Claus. La Belfana goes from house to house, carrying gifts for children, hoping to find the Christ Child.

An old custom in many counries is setting up a cradle scene, or *crèche* (from the French word meaning "cra-

▲ *This very early painting shows one of Jesus' miracles. He is making a blind beggar see again.*

▲ *Mary Baker Eddy, the founder of the religion called Christian Science.*

▲ *A plump, happy Santa Claus, bearing gifts for the children of the world, drawn by the cartoonist Thomas Nast.*

▼ *An early French Christmas card. The first Christmas card was made in 1843. By the 1880's popular cards had pictures of angels, children, snowy scenes, and flowers.*

dle" or "manger"), on Christmas Eve, showing the stable in Bethlehem, the infant Jesus, his family, the shepherds, and the angels. On January 6, the figures of the Three Kings are added to the manger scene in some Spanish countries. This day is the Feast of the Three Kings (Los Tres Reyes), a day of gift-giving.

The yule log, an enormous oak log that is kept burning for as long as possible, is another tradition that is hundreds of years old. Burning the yule log is a custom borrowed from the Norsemen of many hundreds of years ago. They burned a log each year to honor their war god, Thor. During the Christmas season lovely old hymns called Christmas carols are sung. The first Christmas card was printed in 1845. Now millions are sent each year. Decorating with fresh evergreens, holly, and mistletoe has been a custom since earliest times, but the first Christmas tree was decorated only about 300 years ago, in Germany.

Christians all over the world celebrate the Christmas season. It is a joyous time, a time for families and friends, a time when the whole world seems to become kind and gentle, and everyone feels "good will toward men."

ALSO READ: HOLIDAY, JESUS CHRIST.

CHROMOSOME see BIOCHEMISTRY, CELL, GENETICS.

CHURCH AND STATE Different religions exist side by side in Canada and the United States. Americans are free to worship God as they choose. Not all peoples in other countries have this right. In some nations, the government limits religious freedom.

The First Amendment of the U.S. Constitution says that Congress may not pass laws about the establishment

▲ *These children, dressed as Mary and Joseph, are taking part in a traditional Christmas pageant. This is just one of the many traditions that are enacted all over the world at Christmas.*

of religion, or laws that prevent people from worshiping as they please.

Freedom to worship with no government interference goes back to America's beginnings. English Puritans seeking religious freedom settled in Massachusetts in the 1600's. Once in control, however, they tried to force their religion and morality on everyone in their communities. Some colonists rebelled and started settlements elsewhere under their own religious leaders. By the time the Constitution was adopted in 1789, the country's founders knew the importance of religious freedom. The U.S. Congress immediately added the Bill of Rights—the first ten Amendments to the Constitution. One purpose of the Bill of Rights was to separate clearly church (religion) from state (government).

Arguments about the separation of church and state still go on today. For example, some people believe that prayers should be said in public schools. Also, *parochial schools* (schools supported by churches) have been asking for government money. Many people say that giving tax money to church schools or permitting prayers in public schools is against the First Amendment.

■ LEARN BY DOING

Can you think of other ways in which church and state overlap? Do you think it is all right for public schools to have Christmas programs? Should businesses be forced to close on Sundays? Should we have "In God We Trust" on our coins and bills? Should men be deferred from the draft because of their religious beliefs? Should people be free to criticize other people's religions? These are just a few of the questions about church and state. ■

ALSO READ: BILL OF RIGHTS; CONSTITUTION, UNITED STATES.

CHURCHILL, WINSTON (1874–1965)

"I have nothing to offer but blood, toil, tears, and sweat," said Winston Churchill when he became Prime Minister of Britain in the frightening early days of World War II. But he offered, too, a great mind that led his country through the war. This great statesman was the son of Lord Randolph Churchill, who served in the House of Commons, and Jennie Jerome, an American noted for her beauty.

Young Winston was not a good student. But his work improved when he transferred to the Royal Military College at Sandhurst. He graduated near the top of his class. Churchill went to India as both a soldier and a reporter in 1896. He returned to England three years later to run for Parliament but was defeated. He then went to South Africa to report on the Boer War for a British newspaper. He was imprisoned at Pretoria but later escaped.

Churchill ran for Parliament again in 1900 and won. He became Home Secretary in 1910 and worked his way up through various posts. He became Prime Minister in 1940, when Britain was already at war with Germany. In a memorable speech, given when defeat seemed near for Britain, Churchill rallied his countrymen with these stirring words: "We shall fight on the beaches; we shall fight on the landing-grounds; we shall fight in the fields and in the streets; we shall fight in the hills; we shall never surrender."

His leadership during the war was a great chapter in British history, but Britain wanted a change after the war. Churchill's party was defeated in 1945. He remained in Parliament for the next six years and again became Prime Minister in 1951.

Churchill always found time for writing and painting. Painting remained a hobby, but writing was his second profession. His many books include a history of World War II and the six-volume *History of the English-Speaking Peoples*. Churchill wrote only one novel, called *Savrola*. He won the Nobel Prize for Literature in 1953. That same year he was made a knight and became Sir Winston.

ALSO READ: ENGLISH HISTORY, PRIME MINISTER, WORLD WAR II.

CIBOLA, SEVEN CITIES OF

Finding cities of gold has been the dream of many men. The Spaniards who conquered Mexico heard tales of seven fantastic cities (Cibola) supposedly located in what is now the southwestern United States. Many expeditions set out to search for these imaginary riches. In 1540, the famous explorer Francisco Coronado traveled through what are now the states of Arizona and New Mexico, to hunt for the fabled Seven Cities of Cibola. To his disappointment, Coronado found only Zuni Indian villages of stone, not gold.

ALSO READ: CONQUISTADOR; CORONADO, FRANCISCO; EL DORADO.

In 1963, Churchill was made an honorary citizen of the United States.

▲ *Winston Churchill, British Prime Minister during World War II.*

Winston Churchill's American mother was one quarter Iroquois Indian, so the great man had American-Indian blood in him.

▲ *Rodrigo Díaz de Vivar, the national hero of Spain, is better known by the title "El Cid Campeador"—the Lord Champion.*

▼ *The heart is our most important muscle. It pumps blood around the body through veins and arteries. In an adult person, the heart beats 70 or 80 times a minute until death.*

Right auricle

Right ventricle

CID, EL (1040?–1099) El Cid is one of Spain's most famous folk heroes. He was a real person, but his deeds have been told so many times that it is hard to separate truth from legend.

El Cid's real name was Rodrigo Díaz de Vivar. He was a soldier of fortune—he fought for anybody who paid him to fight. His nickname, *El Cid*, comes from the Arabic word meaning "lord." El Cid became famous while fighting for King Alfonso of Castile against the Moors. (The Moors were members of the Islamic faith living in Spain.) But the king and El Cid quarreled, and the king banished him from Castile.

El Cid then gathered a small army and fought for both Christians and Moors. He took Valencia from the Moors in 1094. For five years he ruled a kingdom that included Valencia and Murcia in the eastern part of Spain. The Moors finally defeated him just before his death in 1099. *The Poem of El Cid*, the national epic of Spain, was written about 1140, showing him as a national hero. A famous play, *Le Cid*, written in French, and an opera with the same name were later written about his deeds, as were many other poems.

ALSO READ: SPANISH HISTORY.

CIRCLE see GEOMETRY.

CIRCULATORY SYSTEM
Blood carries oxygen, hormones, and energy-giving materials to all parts of the body by means of the circulatory system. All living things need some means of distributing nutrients, or food, to cells. This can be done without a circulatory system in very simple animals such as sponges. Sufficient nourishment can reach the cells directly from a central cavity. However, more complex animals need a circulatory system.

Some invertebrate animals, such as the lobster, have a simple type of circulatory system. A simple heart pumps blood. The fluid flows into spaces around the stomach and other important parts of the animal's body. It returns through slits in the wall of the heart and is pumped out again.

The circulatory system of humans and other mammals is much more highly developed. It consists of a complicated pump (the heart) to drive the blood, plus a series of tubes, or blood vessels, through which the blood travels. The blood is carried from the heart through blood vessels called *arteries*. The arteries take blood to all parts of the body. Then the blood returns to the heart through *veins*. This was discovered in the 1600's by the English doctor William Harvey.

The system starts with the heart, which is divided into four compartments. The largest compartment is in the lower left-hand side of the heart. Here, the blood gathers, fresh and bright red. As you will see later, the blood in this compartment has just come from the lungs and is loaded with oxygen, which comes from the air breathed into the lungs. This compartment is the main pumproom of the heart. It pumps 70 to 80 times a minute, thrusting the fresh blood out through the main artery. It pumps faster or slower, depending on the body's need for oxygen. You can feel the heart's pumping action if you put your hand on the left side of your chest. You can also feel the blood moving if you place your fingertips lightly on the outside of your wrist, just below the palm. You will feel a throb called the *pulse*.

The main artery leading out of the heart is called the *aorta*. The aorta soon divides into many other arteries. These arteries take the blood to the large areas of the body, such as the head and legs.

The walls of the arteries are thick, strong, and flexible. The arteries can easily become wider or narrower. These changes affect the flow of blood. Just like a river, blood flows slowly through a large, wide channel. But the blood flows faster when the channnel becomes narrow. When you run or use up a lot of energy, your heart pumps the blood faster to move energy-giving materials through your body more quickly. The arteries also become narrower, and the blood pulses through them at a faster rate.

The arteries divide into smaller and smaller branches in each part of the body. They become a fine network of vessels called *arterioles,* "little arteries," and branch into tiny tubes called *capillaries.* Most of these capillaries are so narrow that only one blood cell at a time can flow through them. Capillary walls are so thin that oxygen carried by red blood cells passes easily through them. The fluid part of the blood carries food to the cells of the body and carries waste away. Blood turns from bright to dark red when it gives up its oxygen. The fluid also picks up waste products, including carbon dioxide, from the cells, and then passes back through capillary walls to the blood. The capillaries gradually join one another to form the veins, and the blood starts back to the heart.

Veins have thinner walls and they are not as flexible as arteries. The blood passes through a series of valves, or flaps, in the larger veins. The valves open in the direction of the flowing blood—toward the heart. These valves act like the lock gates of a canal—the blood cannot flow back again once it has passed a valve. The valves keep the flow of blood back to the heart from slowing down. On its way back to the heart, the blood passes through the *liver* and the *kidneys,* which remove the waste matter so that it can be excreted.

The dark red venous blood collects in the upper right-hand compartment when it reaches the heart. It then

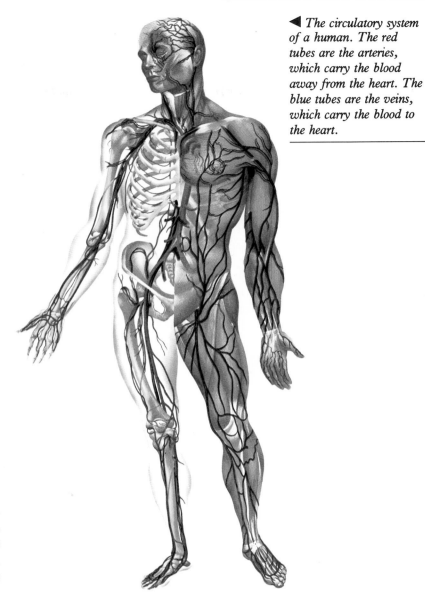

◀ *The circulatory system of a human. The red tubes are the arteries, which carry the blood away from the heart. The blue tubes are the veins, which carry the blood to the heart.*

passes through a valve to a compartment in the heart's lower right-hand side. This chamber pumps the blood to capillaries in the lungs, where carbon dioxide is removed and where the blood picks up a new load of oxygen.

The blood, bright red again, returns to the heart. It collects in the upper left-hand compartment. The blood then passes through another valve into the heart's main pumping chamber—soon to be pumped out once again.

ALSO READ: BLOOD, BREATHING, CARBOHYDRATE, CELL, DIGESTION, HEART, HORMONE, KIDNEY, LIVER, OXYGEN, RESPIRATION.

Your heart beats about 100,000 times every 24 hours, and it pushes your blood through 60,000 to 100,000 miles (97,000 to 160,000 km) of blood vessels.

551

▲ *An old poster of a snarling, angry tiger advertises the most famous circus in America. For many people, the circus is still the greatest show on earth.*

CIRCUS For many years, the circus has provided great family entertainment. The circus came to town announced by a grand parade. Colorful horse-drawn wagons covered with gold leaf and bright paint, marching bands, huge elephants, prancing horses, leaping and tumbling clowns, and wild animals pacing their cages were all part of the parade. The noisy calliope (a musical instrument made of many steam whistles) brought up the rear, spewing out black smoke and gay music. Many children dreamed of running away and joining the circus.

The earliest circuses were held outdoors. Canvas tents were first used in the early 1800's. Separate tents were used for eating, for the trained animals, and for the *sideshow* (the exhibition of strange people such as the bearded lady, the rubber man, and the sword swallower). The *menagerie* tent held rare animals, perhaps a hippopotamus, a giraffe, and a rhinoceros. These animals did not perform—they were zoo animals, just to be looked at. The main show was held in the largest tent, known as the "big top." Few circuses today use tents because of the fire hazard. Most now perform in stadiums or large indoor areas.

Modern circuses usually have three rings, and so much is going on at once that it is difficult to see it all. Acrobats perform in one ring, trained dogs or seals show off in another, while in the third, bareback riders on prancing horses race in circles. High above, aerial artists perform.

After the last show, workers called *roustabouts* begin their job of moving the circus quickly, in order to arrive at the place of the next performance on time. The elaborate scenery must be taken down. The props and all the equipment must be packed up. And everything—scenery, props, animals, and performers—must be loaded on trucks or tractor trailers ready to go.

History Parts of the modern circus came from the ancient Egyptians and Romans, who enjoyed watching acrobats, jugglers, and trained animals. The Romans even used the word "circus," meaning "ring." One huge Roman arena, the *Circus Maximus*, held more than 180,000 people. Chariot races and many other kinds of entertainments were held there.

Jugglers, acrobats, musicians, and tightrope walkers wandered from village to village during the late Middle Ages. They would put on a show or two, collect as much money as they could, and then move on.

Modern circuses began in England and France in the mid-1700's. An Englishman named John Ricketts put on the first circus in the United States in Philadelphia, Pennsylvania, in 1792. President George Washington enjoyed Ricketts's circus very much. Many other circuses were formed in the 1800's. Phineas Barnum was one of the greatest circus owners. Barnum joined forces with another noted circus man, James A. Bailey, about 1880. Their Barnum & Bailey Circus became known as "The Greatest Show on Earth."

Between the late 1800's and the

▲ *Trumpets sound and drums roll as a crowd thrills to see the performing horses under the bright lights of the big top.*

early 1900's, the circus world thrived. The most famous of all circus names was Ringling. The five Ringling brothers started their circus in 1884. They bought the circus of their main rival, Barnum & Bailey, in 1907. The two circuses performed separately for a few years. They were combined into an enormous show, *The Ringling Brothers and Barnum & Bailey Circus*, in 1919. In 1929, America suffered a great business depression. People had no money for amusements. Circuses could not afford to pay their workers or feed their animals, and many circuses went out of business. Today Ringling Brothers—Barnum and Bailey Circus is still the greatest of them all.

Circus Folk and Circus Towns People who work for the circus are proud of their jobs. The performers practice constantly. Most circus acts require great skill and years of training. The animals must be exercised daily. But even the circus must sometimes rest. Several towns in the United States have become famous as winter headquarters for circus folk. Bridgeport, Connecticut, and Baraboo, Wisconsin, were once circus towns. Today Venice, Florida, is home for many circus people. Sarasota, Florida, near Venice, and Baraboo have circus museums. Winter headquarters are where performers practice old acts and work out new ones, fix up costumes, train new animals, and rest. Because soon it will be

▼ *The excitement of the circus is eased by the clowns. By making people laugh, they help them to relax.*

The Ringling Brothers and Barnum & Bailey Circus was so large in the 1920's that it traveled from town to town in 89 double-length railway cars.

Citizenship Day has been celebrated on September 17 every year since 1952. This date marks the signing of the Constitution in 1787. Ceremonies held on that day sometimes honor newly naturalized American citizens.

time to go on the road again, time for the circus!

ALSO READ: ACROBATICS; BARNUM, PHINEAS T.; CALLIOPE; CLOWN.

CITIZENSHIP Have you ever wondered how you became a citizen of the country you live in? People become citizens in several ways. A child is a United States citizen, for example, if his or her parents are U.S. citizens, no matter where the child is born. If only one parent is a U.S. citizen, then the child must live in the United States for five years and request citizenship on his or her twenty-first birthday. A child born on U.S. soil may become a U.S. citizen even if his or her parents are not.

People who leave the country of which they are citizens and who move (emigrate) to another country can usually become citizens of their new home through the process called *naturalization*. People who wish to become naturalized U.S. citizens must meet certain requirements. (1) They must be at least 18 years old. (2) They must have lived in the United States for at least five years and in the state where they are applying for citizenship for the final six months. (3) They must speak, read, and write English, and must know about the history, the Constitution, and the government of

the United States. (4) They must have no criminal record. (5) They must have entered the U.S. legally.

The naturalization laws of the United States now apply to all *aliens* (noncitizens). The first law, passed in 1790, limited naturalization to "free white persons." Blacks were made eligible in 1870. The Immigration and Naturalization Act of 1952, amended in 1965, eliminated the remaining discrimination and made it possible for Indians, Filipinos, and other nonwhites to become American citizens. Naturalized citizens have all the same rights and privileges as native-born citizens, except for one. Naturalized U.S. citizens cannot be President or Vice President of the United States.

U.S. citizenship may be taken away if a person swears an oath of loyalty or allegiance to a foreign country, becomes a naturalized citizen of a foreign country, serves in the armed forces of another country without first getting the permission of the U.S. government, votes in a foreign political election, gives up American citizenship in the presence of an American officer, such as at an embassy in another country, or commits an act of *treason*, or disloyalty.

Some Rights and Responsibilities
Citizens should register and vote in federal, state, and local elections. In this way, people participate in their government. A good citizen finds out who the candidates are and how they stand on important issues. Citizens can run for public office and can serve on juries.

Other countries have their own laws regulating citizens and aliens. The United Nations organization has made rules to help people of the world live together.

ALSO READ: BILL OF RIGHTS; CIVIL RIGHTS; CONSTITUTION, UNITED STATES; ELECTION; UNITED NATIONS.

▼ *Voting machines at a polling station. Exercizing the right to vote is one of the most important duties of a citizen.*

CITRUS FRUIT Oranges, lemons, limes, tangerines, and grapefruit are the best-known citrus fruits. They grow on trees with shiny leaves that stay green all year. The trees grow in the tropics, but the best fruit is produced in subtropical climates.

Citrus fruits have been known for centuries in China. They spread to the Malay Archipelago and India. Arab traders brought seeds to the Mediterranean in the A.D. 800's. The Crusaders probably introduced citrus fruits to Europe. Columbus stopped at the Canary Islands on his way to America and left some lemon seeds there.

The first commercial orange grove was planted in California in 1841. Since then, the citrus industry has contributed millions of dollars yearly

▲ *The sweet orange was originally native to China.*

to the United States economy. Most citrus fruits are now grown in Georgia, Florida, Texas, California, and Arizona.

The fruits of the citrus group are actually a type of berry, with a tough outer covering, or *rind*, dotted with oil glands. The *pulp* inside the rind is composed of many juice-filled sacs. Oranges must ripen before they are picked, but lemons are best if picked green. The fruits are packed in refrigerated compartments on trains or ships for transport to market. Oranges and grapefruit are eaten fresh or processed into canned or frozen juice or concentrates. Lemon juice is added

to canned and frozen fruits and vegetables to bring out a fresh flavor. Lemon juice on fish lessens the fishy smell and adds flavor.

Citrus fruits are rich in vitamin C (ascorbic acid). Vitamin C keeps gums healthy and builds strong blood vessels. The human body needs a regular supply of vitamin C. Sailors on old sailing ships ate citrus fruits to prevent *scurvy*, a disease caused by lack of vitamin C.

ALSO READ: PLANT KINGDOM, SEEDS AND FRUIT, VITAMINS AND MINERALS.

CITY People first lived together in family bands. These bands gave people protection and companionship as they wandered from place to place hunting for food. When people discovered how to grow crops, many of them chose to stay in one place. The groups got larger and more organized and became small villages. These villages grew into towns and, finally, into cities.

The Growth of Cities Some early cities were formed around forts and shrines to gods. The places were sometimes picked because they had water and good soil for farming, or they were built beside good, natural

▼ *A view of Aigeus-Mortes, a walled city in France. Early cities were often built with walls around them as a defense against invaders.*

▲ *Lemons, like all citrus fruits, are rich in vitamin C.*

▲ *The lemon tree has white flowers and glossy green leaves.*

CITY

harbors, at fords on rivers, or near mountain passes. Such cities existed in Egypt, Mesopotamia, and India about 5,000 years ago. Mesopotamia was a land of many small cities, each with its own ruler, laws, army, and chief god.

At first, farmers brought their goods to the city as a gift to their chief god. Later they started trading these goods for the special services of coppersmiths, brick makers, bakers, and teachers. Libraries, schools, theaters, and law courts appeared in these early cities.

Some ancient Greek cities, including Athens and Sparta, were like little countries. They consisted of the city

▲ *A crowded street in Delhi, India. The city has a population of over five million people.*

THE SPREAD OF A CITY

■ CITY AREAS ■ URBAN AREAS OUTSIDE CITY

CHICAGO IN 1850

CHICAGO IN 1900

CHICAGO IN 1970

CHICAGO IN 1980

itself and the outlying areas and were called *city-states*. The powerful city-state of Rome conquered other cities in ancient Italy, then conquered other countries, and set up the huge Roman Empire.

Many European cities founded by the Romans almost disappeared after the collapse of the Roman Empire. But manufacturing and trade increased in the 11th century, and these cities again became important. Many new cities also sprang up during that century. Other new cities were started during the Industrial Revolution of the 18th and 19th centuries. People by the thousands left their farms and villages to work in factories.

Cities are larger today and have become centers for trade. Big businesses often have their headquarters in them. Cities also have great art museums, large hospitals, many theaters, and sports teams.

Cities have spread out, too. Around the central city, or *urban* area, lie the *suburbs*, areas of homes and shops. Many people who live in the suburbs work in the city. A city and its suburbs make up a *metropolitan area*. More than half of all the people in the

United States now live in metropolitan areas. The cities have spread out so much that in some areas, if you look down from a plane, you can't tell where one city begins and another city ends. Such an area is called a *megalopolis*. The area from just north of Boston, Massachusetts, to just south of Washington, D.C., is a megalopolis. More than 50 million people live in this 600-mile (965-km)-long city belt, which has become known as "Boswash."

Geographers recognize other megalopolitan centers. The Great Lakes megalopolis stretches from Milwaukee to Chicago to Cleveland, and it appears to be reaching as far east as Buffalo and south to Pittsburgh. A triangular area in Texas forms another megalopolis. It includes Austin, Fort Worth, Dallas, Houston, and Galveston. The Gulf of Mexico coastline is rapidly turning into another megalopolis. All these megalopolitan areas may join one another someday.

City Life The orders came from the city's boss—something must be done to ease the traffic problems. He ordered certain streets to be made one-way. He also ordered parking lots. He banned carts from loading and unloading during rush hours.

Who was the man who gave these orders? The mayor of New York or Chicago? No, he was Julius Caesar, emperor of Rome 2,000 years ago. Rome's traffic problem was caused by too many people in the streets, too many horse-drawn chariots, and other carts. The parking lots were ordered for the chariots.

Cities today are still fighting traffic problems. Traffic is a big part of the modern city's life. Hundreds of thousands of people travel into, out of, and around a big city each day. They travel to work, to shop, to play. They use buses and subways that move swiftly between underground stations. They use trains to get into the city and back to suburban homes.

They use ferries and bridges to cross rivers to get to the city. They use planes to fly to the city from other cities. They use taxis. And they use cars. City planners say that cars cause the largest traffic jams and are the city's worst transportation headache. Cars need expensive highways on which to run. And cars pollute the city air with gasoline fumes. But the car is one of the most important ways that people get in and out of a city.

Cities have many problems besides traffic. Air and water are polluted, housing is often poor, and crime is frequent.

Yet the big cities of today are similar in some ways to small towns. A big city is really a group of small towns, called *neighborhoods*. Each of these neighborhoods has houses and apartments where people live. Many of these people know each other quite well. Each neighborhood has its own stores, churches and synagogues, sometimes a park or playground, and usually a school. Each neighborhood has its own "personality."

People seldom get lost in a small town, where a few hundred people live. In a city, where thousands of people live, it is easier to get lost. People themselves do not get lost, but the problems of people do. A student not doing well may not be noticed in a big city school. A poor family with-

▲ *A busy junction on a superhighway in Germany, a country that helped to pioneer fast road links between large cities.*

▲ *Many cities grew up around important water routes. This is Rostock, in East Germany. In the distance are part of the port and the shipyards.*

▲ *A crowded street in modern Tokyo, where buildings are like those of any modern city.*

▼ *The gray squirrel is a familiar sight in city parks.*

get about in small airplanes that can land in a few feet of space. People will also move about in speedy subways. Buses will run a few feet above the ground on cushions of air.

The cities of the future may be covered with huge domes that keep out pollution but let in the sun. Some cities of the future may float high in the air, like giant clouds. Others may be built underneath the sea. How do you think cities should change?

ALSO READ: AIR POLLUTION, CITY WILDLIFE, COMMUNITY, HOUSE, STORES AND SHOPS, SUBURB, SUBWAY, TRAFFIC PLANNING.

out enough heat in an apartment may not be noticed in a city with thousands of apartments.

Many cities today are paying more attention to their neighborhoods as they try to solve the city's problems. Some cities are changing their public school systems to neighborhood control. Problems don't seem to get lost so quickly in a neighborhood.

Building for the Future   Some solutions have been found for the problems cities face. The U.S. Government is helping cities to build new housing more quickly where it is needed. New laws have been passed to make factories stop polluting the air and water.

What will the cities of the future be like? Some city planners say these cities may have few cars. People will

CITY WILDLIFE   How many different kinds of wild animals have you noticed in your city? You have probably seen plenty of pigeons waddling along the sidewalks. Sparrows and starlings often join the pigeons in their constant pecking at crumbs and other bits of food. City parks are homes for several other kinds of birds, and many squirrels scamper across the grass or leap swiftly from tree to tree. In some European cities, storks make their homes in chimney tops.

Another common (but much less pleasant) city creature is the brown rat. Rats thrive in damp, low places, especially sewers and basements. They feed on garbage and even on leather, paper, and cloth. Rats are very dangerous because they spread diseases such as rabies. They may also be covered with insects that carry disease.

These are some of the more familiar wild animals that have adapted to the concrete, metal, and machine environment of the city. But many other kinds of animals, that are not as bold as pigeons and squirrels, can also be found in cities and their suburbs. They usually look for food after dark or early in the morning, when fewer people are around.

The forested areas of parks often provide homes for wild mammals such as raccoons, opossums, skunks, rabbits, woodchucks, field mice, and foxes. Weasels, muskrats, and minks are sometimes found near waterways or swampy areas. During the winter when food is hard to find, many wild mammals even venture into yards and along highways. That is when raccoons knock over garbage cans, squirrels shinny up the poles of bird feeders to get at the delicious sunflower seeds, and field mice dig shallow trenches across lawns, looking for grass roots and flower bulbs. Moles and shrews hibernate, or sleep, through winter. But in the summer, they dig tunnels in parks and lawns, looking for worms, insects, and other tasty meals.

Amphibians and reptiles can also be found in city parks. Patient and careful exploration may reveal a population of frogs, toads, salamanders, turtles, lizards, and snakes. The black snake is usually the largest of city snakes. But poisonous species in the United States, such as coral snakes, rattlesnakes, water moccasins, and copperheads, do manage to exist in parks and yards once in a while. If you find a harmless "city" amphibian or reptile, you may enjoy making a new terrarium home for it. But do not go near a snake unless you are certain it is nonpoisonous.

■ **LEARN BY DOING**

You and your friends might want to explore a nearby park to discover what wild animals live there. Try to make your trip early in the day before the park is too crowded. Take along notebooks to write down what you find. Many of the animals may be hiding, so you probably will not be able to see them all. But if you do a little detective work—looking for tracks and other evidence of animal life—you can learn much about even the most timid city creatures. Watch animals such as birds and squirrels

The common rat will eat almost anything. It is a pest to stored produce, as it often pollutes more than it eats. It is known as a disease-carrier.

carefully. How has their behavior changed through living near people? ■

ALSO READ: ANIMAL TRACKS, BIRD, NATURE STUDY, PIGEON, RODENT.

CIVILIZATION People all over the world live in very different ways. Some groups of people, such as the Tuaregs of Algeria or the Australian aborigines, are *nomads*—people who live in small groups and wander about from place to place, caring for their animals and searching for food. Almost all the people must work. They must take care of the animals, hunt, make tools and weapons, cook, or gather plants. Every nomad family grows its own garden and makes its own clothes.

Other groups of people, however, lead a very different kind of life. Some of the people may live in small villages, but others live in huge cities. And not everyone does the same work. Some people care for animals or raise food. Others are doctors, lawyers, policemen, teachers, and mechanics. Do your mother and father have the same jobs, for example? Or do the fathers of all your friends all do the same work? People who live in a group and perform different jobs are using the idea of *division of labor*. When people live in cities and divide the work among them, living be-

Pigeons have been a part of city life for a long time, feeding on crumbs and nesting high on the sides of buildings.

The United Nations adopted a Universal Declaration of Human Rights in 1948. This so-called "international Magna Carta" declared that all persons are born free and are equal in rights.

In 1959 the United Nations declared that children have special rights. These rights were listed in "The Declaration of the Rights of the Child." This says that children everywhere in the world have the right to:

Be able to grow in a healthy and normal way, free and dignified.

A name and nationality.

Social security.

Special treatment, schooling, and care if handicapped.

Love and understanding.

Free schooling and opportunity to play. Equal opportunity to be everything they can be.

Prompt protection and relief in times of disaster.

Protection against all kinds of neglect, cruelty, and being used by others.

Protection from any kind of unfair treatment because of race or religion.

comes even more complicated. People need to keep records and send messages to other people, which makes writing necessary. These three features, cities, division of labor, and writing, mark most civilizations.

People living in the United States today are part of Western civilization. Many parts of this civilization come from the ancient civilizations of Egypt, Greece, and Rome. From Greece came our ideas about democracy. Much of our system of law has its roots in the laws of ancient Rome. Other very old civilizations grew up in Africa, Asia, and North and South America.

The word "civilization" has another important—and confusing—meaning. You can see this meaning in a phrase such as "Indian civilization," or "Chinese civilization," which really means *culture*—the customs, habits, and all other activities that make up the way of life of all the people of India or of China.

For further information on:
Aspects of Civilization, *see* AGRICULTURE, CITY, COMMUNITY, CULTURE, WRITTEN LANGUAGE.
Famous Civilizations, *see* ANCIENT CIVILIZATIONS; BABYLONIA; BYZANTINE EMPIRE; CARTHAGE; EGYPT, ANCIENT; ETRUSCAN; GREECE, ANCIENT; MESOPOTAMIA; ROME, ANCIENT.

CIVIL RIGHTS You cannot be kept out of a public swimming pool, park, restaurant, or any other public place just because you happen to be black or yellow or white. Or just because you are Catholic, Protestant, or Jewish (or any other religion). Or just because you or your parents or grandparents were born in China, Iran, Germany, or anywhere else. Being allowed to use public places is a civil right of all people who live in the United States. Civil rights are those rights that all people are entitled to and that cannot be taken away be-

cause of a person's race, religion, or national origin. Civil rights in the United States are protected by the U.S. Constitution, by the constitutions of several states, and by many national, state, and local laws.

The basic civil rights are stated in the Bill of Rights—the first ten amendments to the U.S. Constitution. The rights of these amendments, such as freedom of the press and speech, freedom to hold peaceful public meetings, and freedom of religion, are protected by the Federal Government. A state law may be canceled by the federal courts if it interferes with these freedoms. Or the U.S. Congress may pass laws to "kill" the state law. A state law can be enforced until the federal courts decide that the law is illegal or *unconstitutional*.

But the laws that protect civil rights must not conflict with other laws. For example, people in the United States are entitled to freedom of religion. But some religions approve having two wives or husbands at the same time, and other laws make this illegal. A man who marries a woman while he is already married can be sent to jail, even though his religion approves of his actions. Many states had laws requiring people to pay a tax if they wanted to vote in elections. But the U.S. Supreme Court said these laws were unconstitutional. Therefore, states can no longer do this.

The Thirteenth, Fourteenth, and Fifteenth amendments to the U.S. Constitution guarantee freedom from slavery, equal protection under the law, and the right to vote. Other civil rights covered by federal and state laws include the right to a job for which one is qualified, the right to use public transportation, and the right to buy or rent any house or apartment that the person can afford.

ALSO READ: BILL OF RIGHTS; CIVIL RIGHTS MOVEMENT; CONSTITUTION, UNITED STATES.

CIVIL RIGHTS MOVEMENT

Many Americans have been concerned about the civil rights of their fellow Americans. All citizens have civil rights promised in the Constitution and the Bill of Rights. But many Americans, including black people, have often been denied their civil rights. The term "civil rights movement" has come to mean the struggle by blacks to be properly protected by the law. Blacks—and the whites who help them—have sought these rights for a long time. Many people have taken part in this struggle and many kinds of groups have been formed to help win equal rights for everyone. Conditions are better in many ways than ever before, but the struggle is far from over. The history of the people and organizations who began and are carrying on this struggle is the story of the civil rights movement.

The First Step   Soon after the Declaration of Independence was signed, the first groups that tried to end slavery were formed in Pennsylvania, Virginia, New Jersey, Rhode Island, Delaware, Maryland, and Connecticut. It took a long time to win freedom for slaves. Some people gave money to "buy" freedom for slaves. Many slaves were taken to freedom in the North on the Underground Railroad, the name given to the system by which slaves traveled from one place to another. They were usually kept hidden during the day and traveled only at night. Some slaves fought to be free. Nat Turner, a preacher, led a slave revolt in Virginia in 1831.

President Lincoln's Emancipation Proclamation of 1863 freed slaves in the rebelling Confederate states. But it did not guarantee anyone an education, a job, or a place to live. The Thirteenth Amendment to the Constitution made slavery illegal. The Fourteenth and Fifteenth amendments, passed soon after the end of the Civil War, were meant to give blacks full civil rights, especially the right to vote.

During the Reconstruction period (1865–1877), many blacks held important posts in government. Louisiana, South Carolina, and Mississippi had black lieutenant governors, and the speaker of the House in Mississippi was black. The superintendent of public education in Florida was a black man. The South had 22 black representatives. Hiram Revels and Blanche K. Bruce served as senators from Mississippi.

White southerners who resented this black progress formed the Ku Klux Klan (KKK) in 1866. This powerful organization was set up to prevent blacks from voting and exercising other rights. Klan members wearing white sheets and masks with pointed hoods often beat up blacks and public officials. They also burned crosses near the homes of people they wanted to frighten. The KKK was declared illegal in 1869. It did not die out but became a secret organization instead.

Black people all over the United States were being denied their civil rights even though laws were passed to protect them. Congress passed an important civil rights act in 1875. This law guaranteed everyone the

▲ *The statue of Abraham Lincoln at the Lincoln Memorial in Washington, D.C. Though Lincoln freed the slaves, the civil rights movement still goes on.*

▼ *Slaves on a tread-wheel on a plantation in the West Indies. The first slaves were taken from Africa to the New World in 1562 by Sir John Hawkins.*

To Thomas Jefferson, one of the most important of civil rights was freedom of expression and a free press. He said that if it was a question of having a government without newspapers or newspapers without a government, he would choose the latter. Newspapers, he thought, were the guardians of all other liberties. Without free reporting of events and free discussion democracy could not endure.

▼ *President John F. Kennedy was assassinated before his program for civil rights for blacks could be carried out.*

right to use public transportation and the right to attend theaters and other public places of amusement. But whites found many ways to get around this law. As a result, most southern blacks were denied the right to vote and other civil rights. Relations between whites and blacks grew worse and worse. From 1900 on, bloody race riots occurred in South Carolina, Georgia, Ohio, Indiana, Illinois, and Texas.

The Struggle Goes On The U.S. Government did so little to help black people protect their civil rights that many black leaders decided that only they themselves could solve their problems. One of the most important and capable leaders was W. E. B. Du Bois. Another black leader of the time was Booker T. Washington, who thought that if blacks were patient, they would win full rights. Du Bois quarreled with Washington, saying that blacks should demand their rights immediately. A conference of black leaders was called in Niagara Falls, Canada, in 1905. The riots had frightened many white and black leaders. Among the 20 leaders at the meeting were Mary White Ovington, Oswald Garrison Villard, Jane Addams, and Rabbi Stephen Wise. They formed the National Association for the Advancement of Colored People (NAACP). During this same period another organization, the Urban League, was founded. Its purpose was to help black people adjust to life in northern cities. Marcus Garvey organized the Universal Negro Improvement Association at about the same time. He stressed black pride, made up the slogan, "Black is beautiful," and said blacks should return to Africa and build new lives.

Thousands of blacks came to northern cities in search of jobs during World War I. The pattern of segregated housing, whites living in one section and blacks in another,

formed "ghettos" in many cities. Many riots took place when blacks attempted to move into white neighborhoods. One of the best known cases was that of Dr. O. H. Sweet, an outstanding black doctor from Detroit, Michigan. Dr. Sweet returned to this country after several years in Vienna, Austria. He purchased a house in an all-white neighborhood. A mob surrounded the house and stoned it. The people in the house shot at them, and a white man was killed. Dr. Sweet and ten other people were charged with homicide. They were defended by the NAACP, with Clarence Darrow, the famous white trial lawyer, serving as chief counsel. They were found not guilty.

Black people were seriously affected by the Great Depression in the 1930's. Some blacks were appointed to administrative posts in government after Franklin D. Roosevelt was elected President. A civil rights section was added to the Justice Department in 1939 to help blacks with their long-denied rights. Supreme Court rulings in several cases aided the civil rights movement. Laws that prevented blacks from voting in primary elections were declared illegal. Cases involving equal opportunity in education from Maryland, Missouri, Oklahoma, and Georgia were decided favorably by the Supreme Court. Black students were finally admitted to state-supported schools as a result of these decisions. Businesses and labor unions came under attack for excluding blacks from jobs and union membership. A. Philip Randolph, a black man and president and founder of the Brotherhood of Sleeping Car Porters, threatened a march on Washington as a protest against unfair labor practices. President Roosevelt then issued an executive order creating a Federal Fair Employment Practices Committee. After President Roosevelt's death, President Harry S. Truman created the President's Committee on Civil Rights to speed progress. This

▲ *The civil rights marches in Washington, D.C. showed the power of peaceful protest.*

action was urged by civil rights groups, including the Anti-Defamation League.

Modern Events Many laws and court decisions regarding civil rights have been passed during the last few decades. Mary Church Terrell was refused service at a restaurant. She filed a suit against the restaurant, and the Supreme Court ruled in 1953 that discrimination and segregation in public places are unlawful.

The Supreme Court heard the most important civil rights case, *Brown* v. *the Board of Education*. In this 1954 case, the Court ruled that "separate but equal" schools were *not* really equal. Many parts of the country had separate schools for black students. Black students forced to attend segregated schools were being deprived of the equal rights guaranteed them in the Constitution. The Supreme Court said this was illegal. This began the period of *school desegregation* which has lasted several years.

In 1955, Mrs. Rosa Parks, a black woman, refused to give up her seat on a Montgomery, Alabama, bus to a white man. She was arrested. Black people were angry, and the "Montgomery Bus Boycott" was launched. No blacks rode the buses, and the city lost so much money that the law was discarded. Blacks could sit anywhere, just as whites could. During the boycott, Dr. Martin Luther King, Jr., head of the Southern Christian Leadership Conference, became an important black leader. Dr. King followed the doctrine of Gandhi, the Indian leader, in urging nonviolence. Dr. King became world famous and received the Nobel Peace Prize for his efforts at bringing together all peoples. He was assassinated on April 4, 1968, and race riots broke out in 50 cities across the United States, as blacks expressed their anger and frustration.

President John F. Kennedy created the President's Committee on Equal Employment Opportunity. Vice President Lyndon Johnson was chairman. Later Thurgood Marshall, former NAACP Legal Defense Fund head and the great-grandson of a slave, was appointed to the Supreme Court by President Johnson. Marshall was the first black Supreme Court Justice. President Johnson also appointed the first black to become a member of a U.S. President's Cabinet, Dr. Robert Weaver, Secretary of Housing and Urban Development.

Next Steps Blacks are winning civil rights. Today, many other minority groups in the United States are involved in the civil rights movement. Many persons are working to eliminate discrimination and to guarantee equal rights and opportunities for blacks, Spanish-speaking Americans, Jews, Orientals, Indians, immigrants, and others. Progress sometimes seems slow to these groups, but much civil rights legislation has been enacted.

Leaders, black and white, sometimes differ on how to win civil rights. Some think they can be won peace-

The high point of the Civil Rights movement was probably the great demonstration in Washington D.C. in August 1963. Over 200,000 people attended the demonstration in support of black demands for human rights. The highlight was a speech by Dr. Martin Luther King, in which he said: "I have a dream that this nation will rise up and live out the true meaning of its creed, 'We hold these truths to be self-evident: that all men are created equal.' "

▲ *Martin Luther King, Jr. preached nonviolence in his campaign for equal rights for blacks. He was awarded the Nobel Peace Prize for his work in 1964.*

When the Civil War broke out, President Lincoln thought that he would need only 75,000 volunteers to put down the Southern uprising in three months. In the end, four million men fought in a war that went on for four years.

▲ *The battle flag of the Confederate Army during the Civil War.*

fully, while others, called *militants*, say that years of peaceful struggle have not worked and that rights must be seized—by violence, if necessary. No one knows what direction the civil rights movement will take next. But it will probably continue to seek equal rights for all under the promise of the Declaration of Independence, "We hold these truths to be self-evident, that all men are created equal, that they are endowed by their Creator with certain unalienable rights, that among these are Life, Liberty, and the Pursuit of Happiness."

ALSO READ: BILL OF RIGHTS; BLACK AMERICANS; CIVIL RIGHTS; CONSTITUTION, UNITED STATES; HISPANIC AMERICANS; INDIANS, AMERICAN; RECONSTRUCTION; WOMEN'S RIGHTS.

CIVIL SERVICE The business of government calls for many skills. Many people are needed to carry out the day-to-day work of government. People who work for the Federal Government belong to the civil service.

Nations have had some form of civil service since ancient times. In China, for instance, government officials were selected under a merit system. To join the civil service, a candidate had to pass an examination. The merit system is the best way of selecting the best-qualified person for each job. It is the system used in the modern civil service to pick people seeking a government career.

This was not always so. When Andrew Jackson became president in 1829, many government workers lost their jobs. They were replaced by Jackson supporters. This kind of thing went on until the passing of the Civil Service Act in 1883. The new law made it illegal to fire or demote a civil service employee for political reasons. It also called for examinations open to all citizens, to select the best-qualified people.

Today more than 85 percent of government jobs come under the civil service law. Exceptions are employees of the courts and uniformed members of the armed forces. In the United States and Canada, the merit system is also used to select civil service employees in state, county, and city government.

The U.S. Government employs nearly three million civilians (nonmilitary people) throughout the United States and the world. A U.S. Government worker might be an agent for the Federal Bureau of Investigation (FBI), a technician at a space center, or a librarian in Japan!

ALSO READ: UNITED STATES GOVERNMENT.

CIVIL WAR The Civil War was fought between 11 Southern states and the United States Government from 1861 to 1865. The two sections of the country clashed over two issues. One was the extension of slavery into the territory of the United States not yet organized into states. The other question was states' rights. People living in the two sections of the country disagreed over how the Federal Government should exercise its powers granted by the Constitution.

The Origins of the War Before the war, many Southerners owned slaves. These slaves were black men, women, and children whose ancestors had been brought from Africa beginning in the 1600's. They worked in the cotton plantations, tobacco fields, and homes of the South.

Slavery was practiced for a time in the North, but the practice died out mainly because slaves were not economical there. Most Southerners, however, felt that slaves were essential for working large cotton and tobacco plantations. They believed their economy would collapse if they had to give up their slaves.

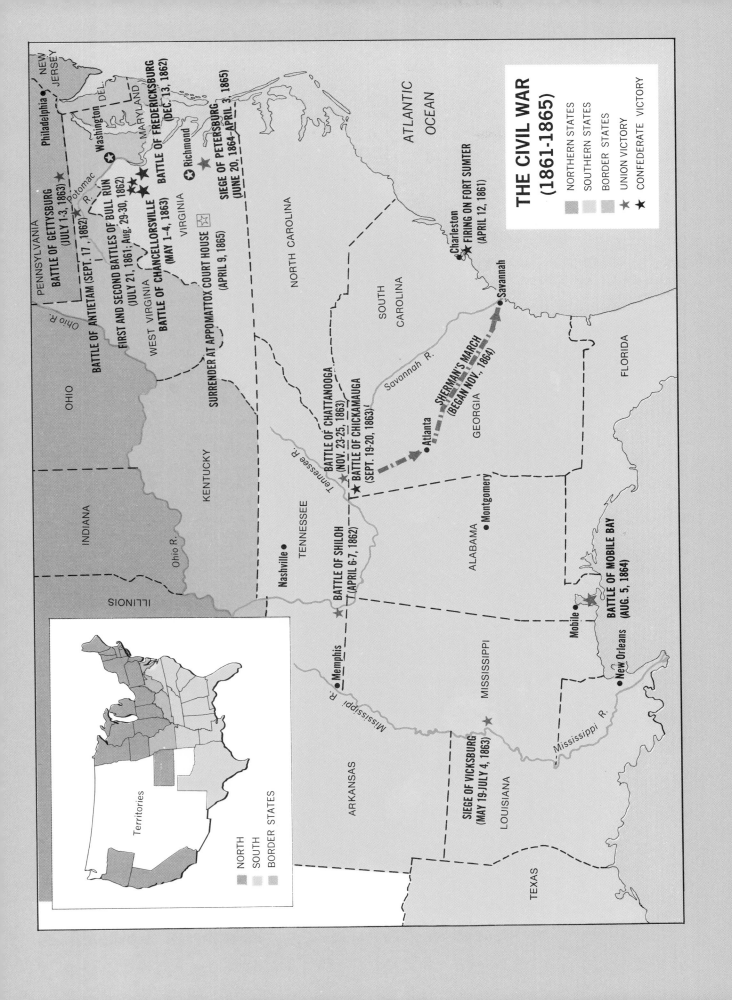

THE CIVIL WAR (1861-1865)

NORTHERN STATES
SOUTHERN STATES
BORDER STATES
UNION VICTORY
CONFEDERATE VICTORY

FIRING ON FORT SUMTER (APRIL 12, 1861)

Charleston

Savannah

SHERMAN'S MARCH (BEGAN NOV., 1864)

Savannah R.

SOUTH CAROLINA

NORTH CAROLINA

ATLANTIC OCEAN

FLORIDA

GEORGIA

Atlanta

Montgomery

ALABAMA

BATTLE OF CHATTANOOGA (NOV. 23-25, 1863)

BATTLE OF CHICKAMAUGA (SEPT. 19-20, 1863)

Tennessee R.

TENNESSEE

Nashville

KENTUCKY

BATTLE OF SHILOH (APRIL 6-7, 1862)

Ohio R.

INDIANA

OHIO

ILLINOIS

Ohio R.

Potomac R.

WEST VIRGINIA

VIRGINIA

Richmond

SURRENDER AT APPOMATTOX COURT HOUSE (APRIL 9, 1865)

SIEGE OF PETERSBURG (JUNE 20, 1864–APRIL 3, 1865)

BATTLE OF CHANCELLORSVILLE (MAY 1-4, 1863)

BATTLE OF FREDERICKSBURG (DEC. 13, 1862)

Washington

MARYLAND

DEL.

Philadelphia

NEW JERSEY

PENNSYLVANIA

BATTLE OF GETTYSBURG (JULY 1-3, 1863)

BATTLE OF ANTIETAM (SEPT. 17, 1862)

FIRST AND SECOND BATTLES OF BULL RUN (JULY 21, 1861; Aug. 29-30, 1862)

Memphis

Mississippi R.

ARKANSAS

MISSISSIPPI

LOUISIANA

Mississippi R.

SIEGE OF VICKSBURG (MAY 19-JULY 4, 1863)

TEXAS

New Orleans

Mobile

BATTLE OF MOBILE BAY (AUG. 5, 1864)

NORTH
SOUTH
BORDER STATES

Territories

▲ *The first naval battle between ironclads was in 1862 during the Civil War. The* Merrimack *was a wooden frigate converted by the South into an armored ram. The North's* Monitor *had a revolving turret.*

▼ *Robert E. Lee was a brilliant general, respected by his fellow officers on both sides, Union and Confederate.*

During the 1830's, 1840's, and 1850's, Americans grew bitter over the slavery issue. The Abolitionists, a group of Northerners, worked hard to end slavery. They stirred up people wherever they could to show the evils of slave-holding. Southerners grew more and more disturbed by Northern attacks on their customs and way of life. They were angered by the Northerners' attempts to prevent them from taking slaves to U.S. territory in the West. They felt at last that they had to withdraw from the United States. They decided to form their own country, where they would be free to govern themselves.

Many historians today feel that there were several other important causes of the war in addition to slavery. One was economic rivalry between the agricultural South and the industrial North. Another was the Industrial Revolution, which changed the nature of farming and manufacturing in both regions.

The crisis came to a climax in the Presidential election of 1860. Abraham Lincoln, candidate of the new Republican Party, was against allowing slavery to spread to the newly settled territories. When Lincoln was elected in November, many Southerners felt they could no longer stay in the Union. They feared that Lincoln would try to interfere with slavery in their states.

Between December 1860 and February 1861, seven southern states voted to *secede*—to leave the United States and form their own nation, or

Confederacy. The states were South Carolina, Mississippi, Florida, Alabama, Georgia, Louisiana, and Texas. They established their capital at Montgomery, Alabama.

The War Begins The North and the South grew tense. On April 12, 1861, the Confederate forces attacked Fort Sumter in the harbor of Charleston, South Carolina. The Fort was occupied by Union troops, but the Confederates wanted it to be in southern hands.

The attack on Fort Sumter caused Lincoln to issue a proclamation calling for 75,000 volunteers to fight to keep the South in the Union. The war was on. Four more Southern states, Virginia, Arkansas, North Carolina, and Tennessee, seceded and joined the Confederacy. Richmond, Virginia, became the new capital. The 11 states of the Confederacy contained about 9 million people, of whom 3½ million were slaves. The western part of Virginia voted to remain loyal to the Union and in 1863 became the separate state of West Virginia.

Twenty-three states stayed in the Union. Four of these were border states, between the North and the South, where slavery was legal. They were Delaware, Maryland, Ken-

▼ *Four Union artillery officers grouped around a cannon near Fair Oaks, Virginia, in June 1862, during the early part of the war.*

tucky, and Missouri. At the time of the war, the only states that existed west of the Mississippi—other than Texas—were Iowa, Minnesota, Kansas, Oregon, and California. All remained in the Union. The 23 Union states contained about 23 million people.

The North had most of the advantages in fighting the war. It had more than twice the total population of the South. It had three times the number of soldiers. It owned practically all the merchant and naval shipping. It had nine times the number of industrial plants, twice the number of railroad lines, and most of the developed mineral resources.

But the South had some advantages, too. It had a greater number of capable military leaders. The Southern soldiers were fighting for their own homes and freedoms. Since most of the war was fought in the South, Southern soldiers were fighting for their land on familiar territory.

The great Confederate generals were men such as Robert E. Lee, Thomas J. ("Stonewall") Jackson, Albert Sidney Johnston, Jubal Early, J. E. B. ("Jeb") Stuart. Lee, a colonel in the U.S. Army until the war, was perhaps the greatest military man of his time. He was first offered the field command of the Union army by Lincoln, but Lee refused because he wanted to remain loyal to his native Virginia and to the Confederacy.

The important Union generals were George B. McClellan, William T. Sherman, Philip H. Sheridan, and Ulysses S. Grant. Lincoln had to change command many times during the war. He finally settled on Grant as the most able military leader.

President Lincoln and his war cabinet used a plan devised by General Winfield Scott to win the war. One branch of the Union army would move west and then down the Mississippi. It would control the river and cut off Arkansas, Louisiana, and Texas. Another branch, the Army of the Potomac, would sweep down the Atlantic states, capturing Virginia and the Carolinas. Then the armies would move together in a "pincers movement" through Georgia, Alabama, and Mississippi.

Important Battles The North suffered the first defeats of the war. The first great battle, the first Battle of Bull Run, took place in July 1861, near Manassas, Virginia. The Union troops were commanded by General Irwin McDowell. The Southern soldiers were led by General P. G. T. Beauregard. The North thought it could easily move through Virginia and capture Richmond. But the South put up such a stiff battle at Manassas that the inexperienced Union forces turned and fled back to

▲ *Uniforms worn by Union (top) and Confederate soldiers during the Civil War.*

◄ *A photograph by Mathew Brady. The Civil War was the first war to be photographed.*

▲ *President Lincoln visits General George McClellan at Antietam Creek, Maryland. Union and Confederate armies battled here on the bloodiest single day of the war, September 17, 1862.*

Washington. The North suffered about 2,900 casualties, and the Confederates lost about 2,000 men.

Another of the great battles early in the war was fought in the West. In Tennessee, on the march to the Mississippi, the opponents clashed in the grim Battle of Shiloh in April 1862. In this fight the Confederate commander of all western troops, General Albert Sidney Johnston, was fatally wounded. The North won, but it was not an easy victory. The Union lost more than 13,000 men, while the Confederacy lost 10,700. Both sides now realized it would be a long and bloody war.

The two forces clashed in the second Battle of Bull Run in the summer of 1862. The South again pushed the

North back to Washington. This time General Robert E. Lee decided to follow up his victory. He pushed into Maryland on his first invasion of the North.

The Confederates got as far as northern Maryland. Union troops dug in at the Antietam Creek, near Sharpsburg. The two armies fought there, on September 17, 1862, on the bloodiest single day of the entire war. The South lost more than 10,000 men on that day, and the North more than 12,000. But the Union stopped the Confederates, and the first invasion of the North failed.

Lincoln issued the Emancipation Proclamation on January 1, 1863. The edict stated that all slaves in those states in rebellion against the United States were to be freed.

A series of battles followed in Virginia and the West. General Lee decided again to invade the North in the summer of 1863. He wanted to move the fighting from Virginian soil because the land was being devastated. This time he reached as far as Gettysburg, Pennsylvania. The two armies met there with disastrous results. The battle lasted for three days, July 1 to July 3, and 43,000 men were killed or wounded. The North suffered 23,000 casualties and the South 20,000. Historians call this battle the turning point of the war, because the Union had stopped the invasion and Confederate losses were so great that the Southern army could never again start a major attack on the North. President Lincoln went to Gettysburg later that year to dedicate a cemetery for the dead of both sides.

The war continued through 1863 and 1864. The North held at Gettysburg. Meanwhile General Grant won his great campaign at Vicksburg on the Mississippi River—thus securing the mighty river for its entire course. The western forces of the Union then pushed from Vicksburg to Tennessee, fighting battles at Chickamauga and Chattanooga.

▼ *The Gatling gun, first used during the Civil War, was a forerunner of the machine gun. Its barrels fired in succession as the handle was cranked.*

Lincoln made Grant commander of all Union armies in March 1864. Grant came east and began to move the Army of the Potomac toward Richmond in the final Virginia campaign. General Sherman, meanwhile, continued to cut across the South toward Atlanta and Savannah, Georgia. He burned and destroyed tons of food, supplies, and equipment in his fast 300-mile (480-km) march from Atlanta to the sea. This act of total war helped strangle the South economically. The Union's plan was succeeding.

Lincoln was reelected in November 1864. At his second inauguration, March 4, 1865, he told how he would seek the peace. "With malice toward none; with charity for all; with firmness in the right, as God gives us to see the right, let us strive on to finish the work we are in; to bind up the nation's wounds. . .to do all which may achieve and cherish a just and lasting peace, among ourselves, and with all nations."

The War Ends Grant's men defeated Lee's weakened army near Richmond, on April 1, 1865. Lee retreated but was caught between Grant and the army of General Philip Sheridan. At the Appomattox Court House in Virginia, General Robert E. Lee surrendered to General Grant. The war was over.

Five days later, on April 14, 1865, a war-weary President went to the theater to relax after the long struggle. In Ford's Theater, an actor, John Wilkes Booth, assassinated Abraham Lincoln. The President did not live to see peace return to his land.

Slavery was finally abolished in all states and territories by the Thirteenth Amendment to the Constitution. The new law took effect on December 18, 1865.

For further information on:

Background, *see* ABOLITION, BLACK AMERICANS, CONFEDERATE STATES OF AMERICA, EMANCIPATION PROCLAMATION, FORT SUMTER, GETTYSBURG ADDRESS, MASON-DIXON LINE, MONITOR AND MERRIMACK, RECONSTRUCTION, SLAVERY, STATES' RIGHTS, UNDERGROUND RAILROAD.

Military Leaders, *see* FARRAGUT, DAVID; GRANT, ULYSSES SIMPSON; JACKSON, STONEWALL; LEE, ROBERT E.; SHERMAN, WILLIAM T.

Other Important People, *see* BARTON, CLARA; BROWN, JOHN; BUCHANAN, JAMES; DAVIS, JEFFERSON; DOUGLAS, STEPHEN A.; LINCOLN, ABRAHAM; STOWE, HARRIET BEECHER.

Some Civil War battles have two names. Northerners named battles after streams, Southerners after communities. Northerners call the Battle of Manassas (town) the Battle of Bull Run (creek). Southerners call the Battle of Antietam (creek) the Battle of Sharpsburg (town).

◄ *A Confederate charge during the Battle of Gettysburg in 1863. The battle was costly and indecisive, but it proved to be the turning point in the war. Less than two years later, in April 1865, Lee surrendered to Grant at Appomattox Courthouse.*

▲ *Oysters lying in their natural habitat—cemented to stones on the seabed.*

▲ *George Rogers Clark, a hero of the American Revolution.*

CLAMS AND OYSTERS Most of the world's seas, and some of its lakes and freshwater rivers, are homes for clams and oysters. There are many different kinds, but the ones we know best are used as food.

Clams, oysters, and their relatives belong to a group of soft-bodied animals called *mollusks*. Like most mollusks, they have protective shells. The shells of both clams and oysters have two tight-fitting sides or valves, so they are called *bivalve* mollusks. New layers are constantly added to the shell as the animal grows. It is possible to trace growth by examining the ridges on the outside of the shell. The sides are hinged at one end and fastened together by a tough ligament. A muscle pulls them shut when danger threatens.

Most clams burrow in sandy or muddy bottoms in shallow water, using a strong, hatchet-shaped, muscular organ called a foot. A hollow tube, or *siphon*, sucks in water, which carries food and oxygen through the soft, fleshy body. A second siphon squirts the water out.

Favorite market clams are the soft-shell, or long-necked, clam and the hard-shell quahog, both from the Atlantic Ocean. The world's biggest clam, found in the Pacific Ocean, has

▼ *The giant clam, like all bivalve mollusks, opens its shell to feed. It may weigh hundreds of pounds.*

a shell that may weigh 500 pounds (225 kg). Scallops are clams with the ability to swim by clapping their shell valves together repeatedly.

Oysters differ from clams in several ways. They have no foot. They cannot move around as clams do. Baby oysters swim freely for a few weeks after hatching from eggs. They then settle on something hard, usually in shallow tidal waters. The oysters cement their tough shells to the object. They remain there for their entire lives, waiting for currents to bring their food and growing about an inch (2.5 cm) a year until fully grown. Large numbers of them settle in beds from Maine to Florida and along the west coast of the United States. Some of the largest beds are in Chesapeake Bay.

Since prehistoric times, oysters and clams have served man as food and in other ways. American Indians carved shell-money, or *wampum*, from the shell of the quahog. Buttons are made from the shells of some mussels. Guess what a person might find in a *pearl* oyster.

ALSO READ: MOLLUSK, PEARL.

CLARK, GEORGE ROGERS (1752–1818) During the American Revolution, Clark led a group of men through the wilderness of the Ohio River Valley. His victories against the British there enabled the United States to claim this valuable region.

Clark was born in Virginia. As a young man he hunted, cut new trails through the forests, and explored the rivers of Kentucky by canoe.

When the Revolution started, he was commissioned an army major. The Ohio valley belonged to the British at that time. Clark knew the land was valuable and that the British forts were dangerous to the revolutionary army. He decided to attack the British, even though he had to use his own money to pay his soldiers. In

1778 he led a force of about 180 men down the Ohio River. They surprised the British and captured the fort at Kaskaskia on the Mississippi River, near where St. Louis now stands. They also took Fort Vincennes and Fort Cook, two important supply bases.

When the peace treaty was signed in 1783, the region north of the Ohio River, called the Northwest Territory, was given to the United States. Five states were later made from the Northwest Territory—Ohio, Indiana, Illinois, Michigan, and Wisconsin.

Clark's younger brother, William (1770–1838), was a co-leader of the Lewis and Clark Expedition.

ALSO READ: AMERICAN REVOLUTION, LEWIS AND CLARK EXPEDITION.

CLAWS AND NAILS

What helps a cat climb high trees, an armadillo dig its way underground very quickly, a swooping eagle grasp a swiftly hopping rabbit? What built-in weapon makes all these animals—and many others—able to survive in the world? The answer to all these questions is claws. Can you imagine any of these animals being able to stay alive very long if their claws were taken away?

Claws and nails are very similar structures. Both are made of hard, nonliving skin cells filled with a tough material called *keratin*. At the base of the claw or nail is a whitish area. On human nails, this area is crescent-shaped, which gives the area the name *lunula* (*luna* is the Latin word for "moon"). The cells in the lunula are living, and as they grow they push the dead cells forward.

Man, apes, and monkeys have nails. Many other animals have claws, nails that are slender, sharp, and usually curved. Hoofs and horns are other special structures that are closely related to claws and nails.

There are two types of claws. One kind is called *retractile*. Retractile claws can be drawn in, pulled back so that the sharp point is protected by *lobes* (little pockets) of skin. All cats—house cats and lions alike—have retractile claws. The cheetah's claws, however, cannot be completely retracted. The second type of claw is short and blunt and cannot be retracted. Dogs, wolves, bears, and some other animals have this type of claw.

ALSO READ: ANIMAL DEFENSES, ANIMAL MOVEMENT, HOOFED ANIMALS, HORNS AND ANTLERS, SKIN.

CLAY see SOIL.

CLAY, HENRY (1777–1852)

"I know no South, no North, no East, no West, to which I owe any allegiance. The Union, sir, is my country." These are the words of the American statesman Henry Clay. He was known as the "Great Pacificator" (peacemaker). In the years before the Civil War, Clay did much to keep the peace between the North and South.

Clay was born in Virginia but moved to Kentucky as a young man. He became a lawyer and was elected to the U.S. Senate in 1806. He worked out the Missouri Compromise in 1820. This law pleased both the North and South, because it allowed Missouri to join the Union as a state where slavery was legal and Maine as a state where slavery was not legal. It also drew a line through the Louisiana Purchase territory. Slavery was allowed only south of that line. Thirty years later, as an old man, Clay helped to keep peace again, helping to work out the Compromise of 1850. California was admitted as a state without slavery, and the territories of Utah and New Mexico were allowed to decide for themselves. Some

CLAWS OF VARIOUS ANIMALS.

Bird of prey

Lizard

Dog

Cat (retractile)

▲ *Henry Clay, the great compromiser, who was a strong believer in the Union.*

▲ *This clay pot, shaped like an animal, was made in China around 2000 B.C.*

historians say that this compromise helped delay the Civil War for ten years.

Clay represented Kentucky in Congress for many years—sometimes as a Senator, sometimes as a Congressman. He ran for President three times but was never elected. It was Clay who said, "I would rather be right than be President."

ALSO READ: CALHOUN, JOHN; JACKSON, ANDREW; WAR OF 1812.

CLAY MODELING How does it feel to squeeze clay in your hands? Clay is not so soft or sticky as mud. When it is wet, you can squeeze or roll it into shapes and figures.

People have been using clay for thousands of years. Even today, our china dishes and bowls are most often made of clay, and so are flowerpots and bricks.

Clay is a type of earth made up of very tiny particles. It is formed from rocks that have been ground down over the ages. In the ground, it looks like very fine-grained mud. It is usually gray or buff-colored, but some clays are red or pure white. Clay is mined in large quantities for industry. You might be able to find some for yourself along the bank of a river or lake. Otherwise, you can buy it in an art store.

Natural clay dries hard, like dried mud. Dried clay is called *greenware*. It is very brittle and breaks easily. Clay pots and figures are usually *fired* (baked) at a very high temperature to prevent breaking. The heat makes the clay as hard as stone. Early man used fires of dried grass and wood to harden clays. Today, special ovens called *kilns* are used for baking clay objects.

All you need for clay modeling is a lump of clay, some water, and a board to work on. You will need to keep the clay quite wet while you are modeling it.

LEARN BY DOING

Salt ceramic can also be used for modeling. Salt ceramic is not a clay but is modeled the same way. Salt ceramic is very clean and gets very hard without firing. You can make salt ceramic in your kitchen. Use a cup of salt, ½ cup of cornstarch, and ¾ cup of cold water. Mix these in a double boiler over heat. Stir constantly until the mixture thickens (a few minutes). Place the salt ceramic in aluminum foil to cool before modeling. ■

ALSO READ: POTTERY AND CHINA, SCULPTURE.

CLEMENS, SAMUEL see TWAIN, MARK.

CLEOPATRA (69 B.C.–30 B.C.) The story of Cleopatra, queen of ancient Egypt, is one of history's most exciting tales. Cleopatra was a cunning, intelligent, ambitious woman. Three times she planned to win control of the Roman Empire. Twice she almost succeeded.

Cleopatra was the last of the Ptolemy family, which ruled Egypt for 300 years. She became queen at the age of 17, sharing the throne with a younger brother, Ptolemy XII. Two years later, in 49 B.C., Ptolemy's guardians seized the throne to gain more power. Cleopatra had to flee. Julius Caesar, the Roman emperor, was in Egypt, and Cleopatra hoped he might help her. She had herself rolled in a rug and delivered to him. Caesar was delighted with this clever plan. He fell in love with Cleopatra and helped her regain the throne.

Cleopatra planned to rule Rome with Caesar, but enemies murdered him in 44 B.C. Mark Antony came to power with Octavian, Caesar's nephew. Mark Antony met Cleopatra and fell in love with her. Together they planned to rule Egypt and the

Roman Empire. Octavian, now Antony's enemy, declared war on them. Octavian defeated Antony's army at Actium in 31 B.C. Antony received a false report that Cleopatra was dead, and he killed himself. Cleopatra tried to charm Octavian, but he resisted. Cleopatra killed herself to avoid being taken prisoner. Legend says that she laid an asp, a kind of snake, on her arm and that the snake's poisonous bite killed her.

ALSO READ: CAESAR, JULIUS; EGYPT, ANCIENT; ROME, ANCIENT.

CLERGY The word "clergy" comes from "clerks." In the early Christian church, clerks were men who served the community as priests. Today the word includes ministers of all Christian denominations, as well as *rabbis*, or ministers of the Jewish religion.

Serving people spiritually is a challenging profession. Clergy must believe and practice the church's teachings. They should be willing to place the community's needs before their own. This takes self-discipline, love for people, and a strong desire to serve them. Most clergy are men, but now more religions are *ordaining* (giving ministerial authority) to women.

Most churches require their clergy to attend a *theological seminary*, or religious training school. The course usually lasts at least three years. It includes Bible study, religious history, and examination of *doctrine*, or beliefs. Modern clergy are also trained in sociology, guidance, and group work. All this preparation helps them to guide people through a wide range of life's problems. Many students in a seminary now do part of their training in inner cities.

Some denominations have rules or customs that shape the personal lives of their clergy. The clergy of the Latin rite of the Roman Catholic Church, for example, may not marry, and the clergy of the Greek Orthodox Church may marry only before they are ordained. Regulations such as these sometimes change as society changes.

Theological seminaries are also changing to keep up with the times. Some have moved from isolated, quiet places in the country to the centers of busy cities, so seminarians can live and study close to the problems of overcrowding and poverty.

ALSO READ: CAREER, RELIGION.

CLEVELAND, GROVER (1837–1908) President Cleveland was the only American President to serve two completely separate terms of office. He was both the twenty-second and the twenty-fourth President of the United States. Between Cleveland's terms, Benjamin Harrison was President.

Stephen Grover Cleveland was one of nine children of a Presbyterian minister. When his father died, Grover had to forget his plans for going to college. At 17 he went to Buffalo, New York, to work as a clerk in a law office. He studied law in his spare time and eventually became a lawyer. He was so honest that people trusted him and elected him to several public offices. He served as mayor of Buffalo and then as governor of New York State.

▼ *Labor problems were a constant worry during Cleveland's Presidency. One of the worst oubreaks of labor unrest occurred at Haymarket Square in Chicago on May 4, 1886. During a strikers' meeting, someone threw a bomb. In the riot that followed, nine people were killed, seven of them policemen.*

Grover Cleveland was the only President to be married in the White House. He and Frances Folsom were wed in the Blue Room on June 2, 1886.

GROVER CLEVELAND

TWENTY-SECOND PRESIDENT   **MARCH 4, 1885—MARCH 4, 1889**
TWENTY-FOURTH PRESIDENT   **MARCH 4, 1893—MARCH 4, 1897**

Born: March 18, 1837, Caldwell, New Jersey
Parents: Richard and Anne Neal Cleveland
Education: Public schools
Religion: Presbyterian
Occupation: Lawyer
Political Party: Democratic
State Represented: New York
Married: 1886 to Frances Folsom (1864–1947)
Children: 3 daughters (1 died at 14); 2 sons
Died: June 24, 1908, Princeton, New Jersey
Buried: Princeton, New Jersey

In Cleveland's time, political "bosses" in both the Democratic and Republican parties often told government officials what to do. But Cleveland believed that his duty was to provide good government for all of the people.

Cleveland continued his policy of honest government when he was elected President in 1884. One hard decision that he had to make as President concerned *tariffs* (taxes on products imported from other countries).

When Cleveland urged Congress to remove tariffs on many articles, American manufacturers became angry. The tariff had protected them from foreign competition. But Cleveland believed the tariffs were too high. He stood by his decision and, as

a result, lost the election of 1888.

Cleveland became President for the second time in 1893. Two months later the country was swept by a financial depression. Many businesses had to close. During a nationwide railway strike, riots broke out among the strikers in Chicago, and Cleveland sent United States troops to restore order. The criticism he received never stopped him from doing his duty as he saw it.

Cleveland's last years were spent in New Jersey, where he taught at Princeton University. Although he was not a popular President, his honesty made him one of the most respected of all American Presidents.

ALSO READ: PRESIDENCY.

▼ *Mesa Verde in southern Colorado is one of the most spectacular examples of cliff dwellings. This cluster of adobe and stone houses was almost impossible to attack from either above or below.*

CLIFF DWELLERS A group of American Indians built amazing houses high in the sides of canyon walls. The cliff dwellings were built between A.D. 1000 and 1200 in Colorado, New Mexico, Arizona, Utah, and northern Mexico. Some of the stone and *adobe* (sun-dried clay brick) houses are preserved as National Parks or Monuments. One of the most famous is Mesa Verde National Park in Colorado.

The cliff dwellers left no written records, but we know many things about their culture. The dry climate of the Southwest has preserved their buildings, tools, clothing, and even food. Archeologists have even found mummies, or preserved bodies.

The tribes began farming the valleys of the Southwest about 2,000 years ago. They grew large crops of corn, squash, beans, and melons, and kept flocks of turkeys. They dug long irrigation ditches through their fields to overcome constant water shortages caused by lack of rainfall. They were skillful carpenters and stone-users, too. Starting around A.D. 700 they made "apartment houses," called *pueblos*, with windows of stone so thin that light could shine through. They built underground ceremonial chambers, called *kivas*, and storage pits for crops.

About A.D. 1000, wandering Indian raiders from the north began to murder field workers, kidnap women, and steal the crops. The pueblo farmers decided to build new homes on ledges or in caves in cliff walls high above the riverbeds. Some were built on the flat tops of mesas. These new apartment houses, made also of stone and adobe, could be reached only by ladders or along paths so steep and narrow that one guard could easily defend them.

The cliff dwellers are believed to have lived in these first "skyscrapers" until about 1350. Then a long and severe drought probably starved them out and forced them to move south. The Zuni, Hopi, and other Pueblo peoples of the Southwest are their descendants.

ALSO READ: INDIANS, AMERICAN; PUEBLO INDIANS.

CLIMATE Temperature, wind, rainfall, sunshine, and humidity (the amount of moisture in the air) are all parts of weather. Weather changes from day to day. But over a long time, weather usually repeats itself. The climate of an area is the usual pattern of weather in that area during a period of many years. For example, the winter is mild and rainy, and the summer is hot and dry in southern California. Some winter days there are cold and dry, and some summer days are cool and rainy. *Usually* the winter is mild and wet and the summer hot and dry. Southern California's pattern of weather is called *dry subtropical Mediterranean climate*.

Climatologists, people who study climate, describe the climates of the world in a number of different ways. The chart on page 576 shows one way.

■ **LEARN BY DOING**
Look at the weather section in your daily newspaper. What was the temperature range in Duluth, Minnesota, yesterday? In Philadelphia, Pennsylvania? In New Orleans, Louisiana? Keep a record of the temperature ranges and the rainfall in these cities for four months. Compare your records with the average conditions in the table to learn which climate each city has. ■

The Making of Climate A climate depends on many things. Among them are latitude, height above sea level, terrain, nearness to an ocean, and ocean currents. None of these

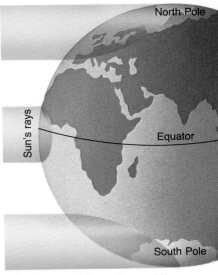

▲ *The atmosphere plays a big part in climate. The less air the sun's rays have to penetrate, the warmer is the place below. The rays must pass through more air and are more thinly spread above the North and South Poles than above the equator. Thus lands nearer the poles are colder than those near the equator.*

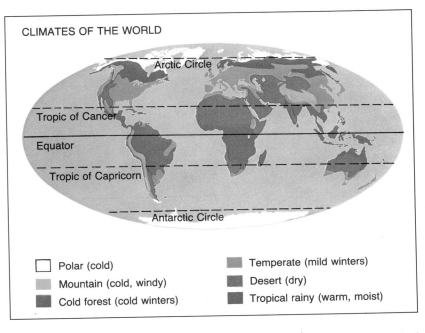

CLIMATES OF THE WORLD

- Polar (cold)
- Mountain (cold, windy)
- Cold forest (cold winters)
- Temperate (mild winters)
- Desert (dry)
- Tropical rainy (warm, moist)

Climate	Usual Weather	Areas That Have This Climate
Polar	Always cold; temperature almost always below freezing. Little rain or snow in any season.	North Polar icecap. Northernmost Alaska, Canada, and Siberia. Greenland. Antarctica.
Subarctic	Long, severely cold winter; short, cool summer. Coldest month below freezing; warmest below 50 degrees F (10°C).	Most of Alaska and Siberia. Central Canada. Northern Sweden, Norway, and Finland.
Wet Continental Short Summer	Very cold, snowy winter; cool summer with some rain. Coldest month below freezing; warmest above 50 degrees F (10°C) but below 72 degrees F (22°C).	Southern Canada east of 100° longitude. Northern United States between Appalachian and Rocky mountains. Upper New England. Most of European Russia. Scandinavia east of Atlantic Coast. Northern Manchuria.
Wet Continental Long Summer (Temperate)	Cold, snowy winter; hot summer. Some rain in every month. Coldest month below freezing; warmest above 72 degrees F (22°C).	Lower Great Lakes and central midwest states. Lower New England states; southern New York; New Jersey.
Wet Subtropical Mild Winter	Occasional frost or snow in winter; hot summer. Rainfall throughout year. Coolest month above freezing, but below 64 degrees F (18°C); warmest above 72 degrees F (22°C).	Southeast United States. Eastern third of the continents between 25° and 40° north and south latitude.
Dry Subtropical Mediterranean	Mild rainy winter; hot dry summer. Coolest month above freezing, but below 64 degrees F (18°C); warmest month above 72 degrees F (22°C).	Most of California. Shores of the Mediterranean Sea. West coast of South America between 30° and 50° latitude.
Desert (dry)	Hot days, cool to cold nights. Rainfall very rare. All months above freezing.	Southern Arizona and New Mexico. Southern California peninsula. Sahara and Kalahari deserts in Africa. Arabian desert in Asia. Coasts of Peru and northern Chile. Eastern Australia.
Wet and Dry Tropical Monsoon	Much rain in summer; dry period in winter. Very warm with little change in temperature from season to season. All months above 64 degrees F (18°C).	Central America. Indochina. Philippine Islands. Southern India. Northern fifth of South America.
Tropical Rainy	Hot and humid all year. Enough rainfall for thick forest growth all year. All months above 72 degrees F (22°C).	Southern tip of Florida. Amazon River Basin in South America. Africa between Sahara and Kalahari deserts. Most of Indonesia. Central India.
Temperate Marine or Marine West Coast	Cool summer, mild winters. Coldest months above freezing, below 64 degrees F (18°C); warmest above 50 degrees F (10°C). Some heavy rain and snow in winter; ranges from 20 to 80 inches (50-200 cm) a year.	Northwestern U.S. coast. British Isles. Denmark. Germany. Netherlands. Belgium. France (except southern coast).

alone makes a climate. Several must act together.

Latitude is distance from the equator. The climate at the equator is the hottest on Earth because the sun's rays shine most directly there. The sun's rays strike the Earth less directly in areas north or south of the equator, so the climate in these lands is cooler.

Mountain tops and high plateaus have cool or cold climates. And winds blow stronger and more often here than in low-lying places.

An area of the Earth's surface may include hills, mountains, or lowlands. The area may be sandy, grassy, marshy, forested, or rocky. These features indicate *terrain*. Some terrains absorb the sun's heat very well, and others absorb poorly. Some give up the absorbed heat quickly, others slowly. The amount of the sun's heat that the terrain of an area can take up and give off plays an important part in climate.

Mountains have a big effect on climate. For example, warm, moist air blowing eastward from the Pacific Ocean must rise to pass over the mountains along the northwest coast of the United States. When the air rises, it cools and drops its moisture as rain. As a result, the western parts of Oregon and Washington have a moist, rainy climate. The air that slides down the eastern side of the mountains is cold and dry—and so is the climate on the eastern side.

Ocean water absorbs the sun's heat slowly and gives it up slowly. Land areas absorb and give off heat more rapidly. In cold weather, the shores of an ocean are warmer than inland areas. Air warmed by contact with the ocean water blows over the coastal areas, warming them. In hot weather, the ocean air is cooler than the air over the land, and the coastal areas are cooled by sea breezes. Also, winds blowing in from an ocean carry moisture that gives coastal areas a wet climate.

Changing Climates Climate can change. It changes slowly over a long time. The northern halves of North America, Europe, and Asia were covered by ice during the period known as the Ice Age. Winds blowing off the ice gave a cold climate to what are now subtropical areas, such as the Gulf States and the shore of the Mediterranean Sea. The ice began to melt about 12,000 years ago. Most of the areas it once covered now have a temperate (mild) climate.

Climate and Your Life The climate in which you live affects the way you live. If you live where winters are cold and windy, you need a solidly built house with a good way of keeping it warm, such as furnace heat. If you live in the tropics, your house need not even have windowpanes nor any way of being heated. People must wear thick clothes in cold climates. They need not wear so many clothes in the tropics.

Eskimos cannot grow crops in a polar climate. They eat meat and blubber. People in Southeast Asia eat much rice, because rice grows well in their wet and dry tropical climate. North Americans and Europeans eat much wheat, corn, and rye, because these crops grow well in their temperate climates.

ALSO READ: HUMIDITY, RAIN AND SNOW, WEATHER, WIND.

CLIVE see INDIA.

CLOCKS AND WATCHES People have had accurate means of measuring time for only a few hundred years. Before that they depended on primitive timepieces such as sundials and water clocks.

■ **LEARN BY DOING**

You can make a time indicator much like those used thousands of years ago. Push an upright stake into a flat piece of ground, where the sun can shine on it all day. You will see that the shadow gradually moves around the stake as the sun moves across the sky. The shadow will be short at midday, when the sun is high. In morning and evening, when the sun is low, the shadow will be much longer.

Before modern clocks were invented, this device, the *sundial*, was used to tell time. It was not very accurate, but at least people knew more than just whether the day was almost over, just beginning or somewhere in the middle. With the aid of a clock or watch, you can mark the positions of the shadow at various times, such as 9 a.m., noon, and 3 p.m. See if your "sun clock" tells the right time three months later. Six months? Nine months? What about after a year? What happens during a year that might explain this? ■

The *water clock* was invented by the ancient Egyptians. A container with a small hole in the bottom was filled with water. The passing of time was marked by the gradual fall of the water level in the container. The Greek name for a water clock was *clepsydra*.

▲ *The sundial is our oldest timekeeper. When the sun is out the sundial's gnomon (pointer) casts a shadow that moves over the lines telling the hours.*

▼ *Early mechanical clocks were driven by a weight on the end of a cord wound around a drum. As the drum rotated, it turned the hands of the clock.*

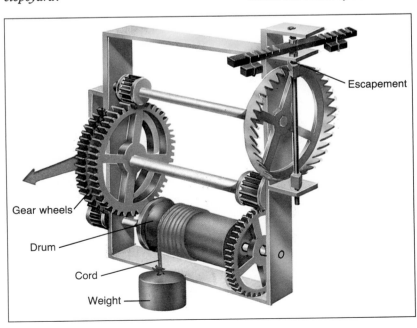

Escapement

Gear wheels

Drum

Cord

Weight

▲ *The stately grandfather clock is driven by the movement of the long pendulum housed in the oblong case.*

▼ *A digital watch shows the time in numbers. Inside is a quartz crystal that vibrates an exact number of times a second.*

The Chinese made the first mechanical clocks in the A.D. 600's. They were water clocks with dials driven by gears. In the 1200's European clockmakers started using falling weights, hung on long cords, to drive clocks. As a weight descends it moves a series of gears, sometimes called cogwheels. The gears move the hands that point to the hours and minutes on the clock face.

To control the rate at which the weights descended clockmakers invented various forms of *escapement*, a mechanism that allows a weight to escape or descend a little bit every second. The speed of escape is controlled by a pendulum, a weight that swings to and fro at a steady rate. The tall clocks known as grandfather clocks are pendulum clocks.

Springs to drive clocks were first used in the 1300's and spring clocks have remained the most common form of clock every since. As the spring uncoils it drives a series of gears, just like those of a weight-driven clock. Most spring clocks have a *balance wheel* instead of a pendulum to control their speed.

Electric clocks first came into general use in the 1920's. They are powered by batteries or regular household electric current. While most of these clocks have a balance wheel or pendulum like older clocks, some have tiny *tuning forks* whose vibrations can be made to turn the machinery that controls the hands of the clock. The vibrations of the tuning forks are controlled by the amount of electricity that reaches them.

Watches are really very small clocks. They used to be carried in pockets. Now they are usually worn on the wrist. Watches are made in the same way as a spring clock. The spring of a watch usually takes 24 hours to unwind. Electric watches have tiny motors powered by very small batteries. A revolution in timekeeping came in the 1960's when electronic watches and clocks first came into general use. The heart of an electronic timepiece is a tiny *quartz crystal*. This crystal vibrates and produces an electric current that is used to power the clock movement. Quartz clocks and watches are extremely accurate, losing or gaining less than one minute every year. They can be made very cheaply, and are increasingly popular. Some watches are combined with miniature calculators.

The most accurate type of clock is the *atomic clock*. These clocks depend on chemical elements that release light and radio waves at a known, constant rate. The twin atomic clocks at the U.S. Naval Research Laboratory are the most accurate measuring devices on Earth. They will gain or lose only one second in 316,000 years!

ALSO READ: BIG BEN, TIME.

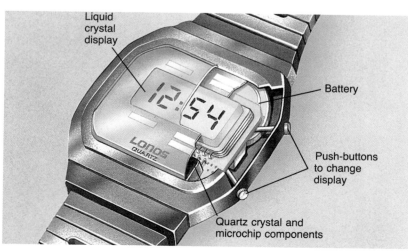

Liquid crystal display

Battery

Push-buttons to change display

Quartz crystal and microchip components

CLOTHING When did people start wearing clothes? Perhaps in some long-ago cave, someone noticed the softness and warmth of the fur of the wild sheep that had been killed and skinned for dinner. They might have put it around their shoulders and realized that it made them feel comfortable in the damp, chilly cave. Meanwhile, Eskimos, Lapps, and other peoples of cold northern regions were discovering that the skins of wolves, bears, reindeer, and other animals could keep people warm.

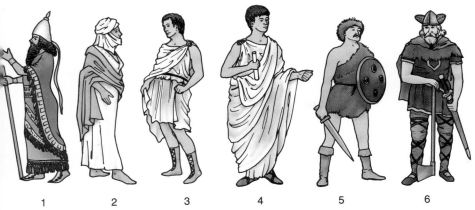

Sometime after that came the idea of connecting two skins together. A piece of animal sinew (connective tissue) could have been left in the cave (or the tent or the igloo) after an animal was skinned. Someone playing with the sinew put it through a hole in one skin and then through a hole in another skin. Two skins were connected together! Later on someone found that putting the sinew through the hole was made easier by using a bone to guide the sinew. This was the beginning of sewing. Once animal skins could be sewn together, people could cover themselves well.

The Eskimos not only fastened skins together. They realized that heat rises, and they learned to make clothing that fits tightly at the top, to keep all the body heat trapped inside. If you wear a parka, which was invented by Eskimos, you know that this hooded coat—with its tight collar and cuffs—can keep you warm longer than any other coat.

Many people lived in parts of the world where it was never cold. They discovered it was good to cover themselves for other reasons—to keep the hot sun from burning their skins and to guard against stinging insects and poisonous plants. Someone discovered how to weave coarse palm fronds (leaves) together to make a kind of body covering. Other people, especially those who lived on sunny islands in the south Pacific Ocean, learned to make cloth by mashing bark, in much the same way as paper is made.

Then someone, perhaps a child sitting on an African riverbank, began twisting the pretty white puffs of a cotton plant between his or her fingers. Maybe the child found that he or she could twist a long thread that way. Someone else found that many of these threads could be woven together to produce cloth. The same discovery was made with the flax plant. Its fibers could be twisted into thread, too, and linen could be woven from the threads. And in China, somebody discovered that the cozy, soft cocoon in which the silkworm changes into an adult moth, can be unwound and twisted into a thread. Someone else wove the soft and delicate material called silk from the thread.

People began to decorate their new discovery—cloth—with bits of shell or pearls or precious bits of the newly discoverd alloy, bronze. They found that they could make the cloth different colors, too. They made earth colors from clay and other soils. They used dye made from the bark of trees and from the juice of berries for other colors.

In cold climates, people who first wore sheepskins found that the wool from a sheepskin could be twisted into threads, and then woven into cloth, as cotton and flax were in warmer places. A man did not have to kill the sheep and skin it. He could

▲ *If you lived in a cold part of the Northern Hemisphere, you would have to bundle up against the cold as this little girl has done. People in many countries embroider their clothing with bright designs.*

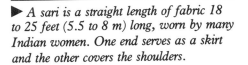

▶ *A sari is a straight length of fabric 18 to 25 feet (5.5 to 8 m) long, worn by many Indian women. One end serves as a skirt and the other covers the shoulders.*

▲ *The miniskirt, created by the British designer Mary Quant in 1965, made women's skirt lengths the shortest ever.*

Needles with eyes have been found in Stone Age caves in Europe. These needles are at least 30,000 years old. They were made from the leg bones of large birds.

The ancient Romans wore shoes of fine leather with silver and gold ornaments. The height of the shoes showed the wearer's rank.

clip the wool off the sheep and let the animal go, or—still better—he could keep the sheep until its wool grew again. Woven wool was warm and comfortable.

People wove cloth pieces in many sizes. Some people in hot climates wove short pieces to be tied at the waist. The Egyptians, who lived in the hot lands along the upper Nile River, liked loose clothes made of cotton. Across the Mediterranean Sea, the Greeks wove wool from the sheep they raised on the mountainsides. As Rome became a powerful civilization, the Romans began to wear a long garment wrapped around the body and thrown over the left shoulder. This was called a *toga*, and a Roman male wore it proudly as a sign of being a Roman citizen.

Roman soldiers wore different clothing to protect themselves in battle. They wore heavy bronze helmets to protect their heads from sharp blows and panels of bronze on their clothing to shield their bodies.

The Romans saw a new kind of clothing when barbarian invaders came from the East. These people rode horseback. They wrapped cloth around each leg to protect their skin from rubbing and to keep from sliding off their sweaty horses. So trousers were invented.

Iron came into use in Europe, and soldiers began using that metal to make protective helmets. A visor was added to the helmet, so a warrior could pull a metal covering down over his face. Other iron pieces were used to shield his body in battle. A soldier's whole body was soon covered by an iron suit that weighted about 70 pounds (30 kg). Knights wore this armor for hundreds of years in combat. It went out of style when guns were invented, because bullets went through the armor.

Europeans were very excited when silk cloth was brought from China. This soft, beautifully colored cloth was very valuable. Kings and queens prized their silk gowns and robes. Europe wanted the silks of the Orient so much that countries fought wars over trading with the East. Columbus dreamed of finding China and its silks as he set off on his voyage of discovery in 1492.

Making cloth was a long, hard process when America was being settled. Most homes had a spinning wheel and a loom. Women were expected to spin yarn into coarse, plain cloth called *homespun*. Many settlers wore clothing sewn from homespun, from underwear to shirts, trousers, and dresses. The colonists raised sheep, and flax and cotton were soon planted in the South. Many colonists, especially on the frontier, imitated the Indians and dressed in buckskin clothes made of the skins of deer.

Clothes for special occasions were often prepared by dressmakers and tailors who traveled from settlement to settlement. Only a few very large cities had permanent tailors and dressmakers. These special clothes had to be measured many times, and they were sewn by hand, which took a very long time. Such clothes were so expensive that only very rich people could afford them.

A great invention made in England at this time was machinery for spinning and weaving. These machines, run by steam, were set up in mills. Thousands and thousands of people went to work in them, and spinning mills became great businesses, first in England and later in the United States. Factory-made cloth made a great change in people's lives. Spinning and weaving in the home were almost forgotten because attractive materials could be made easily and cheaply. Soon other machines were developed that could quickly sew many pieces of clothing. Traveling tailors and dressmakers could not get work because fashionable clothes could be bought in any store for far less money.

The mills brought other changes,

too. Cotton would not grow in England, so the South developed huge cotton plantations to feed Britain's hungry mills. Later, American mills grew larger and bought huge amounts of cotton from southern planters.

A great change came in clothing in the later 1800's when chemists invented rayon, the first man-made fabric. Soon others were developed—nylon, Acrilan, and Dacron, for example. These *synthetic* (man-made) fabrics often wear longer, dry faster, and hold color longer than cotton, silk, linen, or wool.

Sometimes a combination of natural and synthetic fabrics works well. So many people have begun to wear synthetic clothes that less cotton is being grown and fewer sheep are being raised throughout the world. Synthetic clothes are lightweight and easier to carry while traveling.

Several important changes in clothing have occurred recently. Until the 1940's, for example, boys often wore shorts, or "knee pants," all the time. Buying a boys' first pair of pants was a big event that might happen on his twelfth birthday. Girls' clothing has changed, too. Girls' dresses were different from women's dresses. But today most girls' clothing looks like smaller copies of the clothing that their mothers wear.

Men's clothes have also changed in just a few years. Now men can choose heavy, warm suits for winter, and cooler, lighter-weight suits for warmer weather. Also, it has become less important than it used to be to wear jackets, vests, and neckties.

Important changes are going on in women's clothing, too. Until a few decades ago, women never wore shorts or pants. Now women can wear pants to work, just as men do. And many other styles are designed to suit both men and women. These clothes are often called "unisex" clothes ("uni" means "one").

Finally, more different kinds of clothes are made today than ever be-fore. And sports clothes, comfortable casual clothing that wears well, are manufactured just for people to wear for recreation.

For further information on:
Articles of Clothing, *see* BUTTON, FASHION, HAT, JEWELRY, SHOES.
Clothing Materials, *see* COTTON, DYE, FEATHER, FUR, LACE, LEATHER, SYNTHETIC, TEXTILE.
History, *see* ARMOR; INDIANS, AMERICAN.
Making and Caring for Clothes, *see* KNITTING, LAUNDRIES AND DRY CLEANERS, NEEDLEWORK, SEWING, SEWING MACHINE, SPINNING AND WEAVING.

▲ *Much of today's casual clothing is made for comfort and durability. Informal dress for boys and girls is very similar.*

CLOUD   If you ever fly in a plane and suddenly find that strong winds are pushing it every which way and that hailstones are beating against it, you can guess that the pilot could not avoid flying through dark, heavy cumulus clouds. Pilots avoid these cloud banks whenever they can, because inside them they will often find rough weather.

▼ *Clouds form as warm air rises and cools. The water vapor in the air then condenses into droplets to form clouds.*

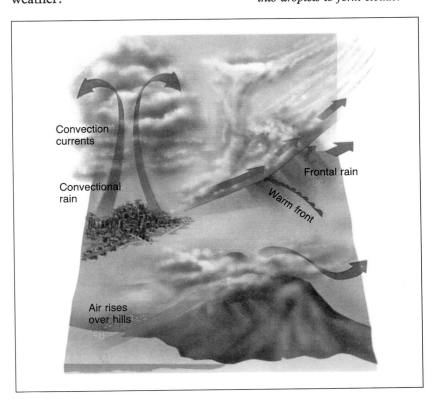

Convection currents

Convectional rain

Frontal rain

Warm front

Air rises over hills

CLOUD

▶ *There are ten main cloud types, grouped according to their height. Five are low (up to 8,000 feet; 2,500 m). They are* stratus, *a uniform gray cloud;* cumulus, *a white puffy cloud;* cumulonimbus, *or thundercloud;* nimbostratus, *a dark cloud often blurred by rain and snow; and* stratocumulus, *a grayish-white shaded sheet of cloud. Medium clouds occur between about 8,000 and 20,000 feet (2,500 and 6,100 m). They are* altocumulus, *a grayish-white rounded cloud; and* altostratus, *a grayish sheet of cloud. High clouds, above 20,000 feet (6,100 m), include* cirrocumulus, *a thin, rounded cloud;* cirrostratus, *a transparent, whitish cloud; and* cirrus, *a delicate, white, fibrous cloud.*

On a cold day, go outside and blow your breath into the air. The water vapor in your breath will condense and form a "cloud." Boil some water in a teakettle. The clear space directly in front of the spout is full of water vapor although you cannot see it. The vapor soon condenses to form a "cloud" a little farther from the spout. In both these instances, you have made clouds!

If you see cumulus clouds in an early-morning summer sky, you can predict that afternoon will bring showers and thunderstorms. Much of the time you will be right. Have you ever wondered about clouds? What are they made of? How do they get into the sky?

Water and Ice in the Air A cloud is a mass of water droplets or very small ice crystals. They are ten thousand to a million times as small as raindrops.

There is always some water in the air, even over the driest desert or in the hottest room in a house. The water is in the air as *water vapor*, water in the form of a gas. The amount of water vapor in the air is known as *humidity*. You cannot see water vapor. Warm air can hold more vapor than the same amount of cool air. Water vapor *condenses*, or changes back to liquid water, as air cools. The condensed vapor forms droplets of water such as those that make up clouds.

Suppose a wind is blowing from the Gulf of Mexico northward across the southeastern United States. The wind—which is a mass of moving air—will be carrying much water vapor, because the air is warm and has just absorbed water from the gulf. Suppose also that cold air, which has just passed over Alaska and Canada, is sliding southward over the northern United States. The two masses of air might meet near southern Ohio and Indiana. The dividing line between the two air masses is called a *front*. Along the front, the cold air will slide under the warm air and push it up. The water vapor in the warm air will condense and form clouds.

Clouds can form when a mass of warm air meets cold air. Air moving upward from the surface of the Earth becomes 5½°F (3°C) colder for every thousand feet it rises. If air rises rapidly to higher than 20,000 feet (6,000 m), the condensing water vapor forms tiny ice crystals instead of water droplets.

Very small solid particles around which the vapor can condense must also be present for clouds to form. Such particles, called *condensation nuclei*, are almost always in the air. They come from dust, pollen, smoke, and sea salt. Solid particles of chemicals can be scattered in the air from planes to make "artificial" rain on a small scale.

Types of Clouds If you have ever looked closely at clouds, you know that they do not all look alike. Clouds are usually named for the type of weather they bring or for the height they are seen at. Clouds that look like layers are *stratus* clouds. Large, fluffy, cottonlike clouds are *cumulus* clouds, These clouds may bring thunderstorms in the summer. Dark, heavy, rain clouds are called *nimbus* clouds. Very high and thin clouds are *cirrus* clouds, which are usually made up mostly of ice crystals.

Clouds and Rain If the temperature of a mass of air continues to lower after clouds have formed, the water droplets become larger and larger. They finally grow so large that they fall to earth as raindrops.

ALSO READ: ATMOSPHERE, CLIMATE, HAIL, LIGHTNING AND THUNDER, RAIN AND SNOW, WEATHER, WIND.

CLOWN The art of clowning has been known for centuries. In the Middle Ages every royal court had a clown, called a *court jester*. It was the jester's job to amuse the king and his court. Clowns have also been called *merry-andrews, fools, buffoons,* and *pantaloons.* Circuses have always had clowns. The first circuses were small. The clowns told jokes and sang songs to the audience. When circuses grew larger, not all the people could hear the clowns, so clowns began to use *pantomime* (acting out scenes silently) and to work in large groups.

There are many different kinds of circus clowns. One of the oldest types is the *whiteface* clown, who paints his or her face with white makeup. The *august* clown has a white face, too, but adds a big red nose and wears baggy pants and enormous, flopping shoes. The *rube* dresses as a funny country farmer, and the *hobo* dresses like a tramp. Still other clowns wear costumes to make them look like cartoon characters or famous people. Each clown creates his or her own makeup. No other clown ever copies it. Clowns use many objects, including some very noisy ones, in their acts. The tiny clown car is a big favorite. Many more clowns come tumbling out of the car than you think could possibly fit inside. Besides making people laugh, a clown must also hold everyone's attention while equipment is being moved about the circus rings. A clown must be highly skilled. He has to be a good actor and acrobat. Many clowns are musicians, too. Ringling Brothers and Barnum & Bailey Circus has a clown school.

Many clowns have been famous. Joseph Grimaldi was a popular European clown in the last century. His nickname, "Joey," has become a slang word for clown. Dan Rice was one of the first great clowns in the United States. He had his own circus, and President Abraham Lincoln often came to watch him perform. Felix Adler was a famous clown who performed with a wonderful trained pig. Millions of children and grown-ups loved Emmett Kelly's sad tramp face.

Other clowns work in ice shows.

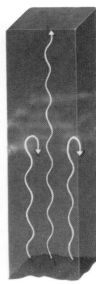

▲ *Clouds act like a blanket, so a cloudy day (left) will stop some of the sun's heat from reaching the Earth. But a cloudy night (right) will keep the Earth's warmth from escaping.*

▼ *Some traditional types of clowns. Front: Auriol; Left to right: The Fool; Gilles; Percy Huxter (whiteface clown); Coco (august); and Little Billy (midget).*

▲ *Clowns perform in colorful water shows at Cypress Gardens near Winter Haven, Florida.*

Fir club moss

Stag's-horn club moss

▲ *Two kinds of club moss. These plants have lived on Earth for hundreds of millions of years.*

584

They are really excellent skaters and acrobats—if they could not skate very well, they would be badly hurt. Still other clowns work in rodeos. These men do a necessary, dangerous job. They protect the cowboys from the powerful Brahman bulls. Only a quick leap over a fence or a headlong dive into a barrel keeps these brave clowns safe.

ALSO READ: CIRCUS, RODEO.

CLUB MOSS Deep in shady forests you may find a small, creeping, mosslike plant with scaly, evergreen leaves, called club moss. It first grew on the earth several hundred million years ago, when club mosses grew to be 100 feet (30 m) tall.

Club moss was once widely used to make Christmas wreaths. However, excessive use of this slow-growing plant has caused it to become scarce in many parts of the United States.

Club moss is a primitive plant closely related to the ferns and horsetails, and is called a *fern ally*. Club moss is considered more advanced than true mosses because it has special groups of cells for conducting food and water.

About two hundred species of club moss are known. They resemble large mosses or small evergreens. Most grow best in the rich leaf mold of a forest, but a few tropical species grow on forest trees like some orchids. Club moss usually trails over the

ground, and it is sometimes called *ground pine* or *running pine*. Club mosses bear *spores* (germ cells), usually on the upper part of their shiny green stalks. The spores are sometimes on separate stalks.

ALSO READ: FERN, MOSSES AND LIVERWORTS, PLANT KINGDOM.

CLUBS AND SOCIETIES It is fun to do things on your own, but sometimes it is more interesting to do things with others. For this reason, you may want to join a club or start your own.

Many national associations of clubs exist for young people of school age. These clubs combine companionship, hobbies, and learning. They include Boy Scouts, Girl Scouts, Camp Fire Girls, Boys' Clubs, Girls' Clubs, 4-H, Future Farmers of America, and Junior Red Cross. Clubs are also sponsored by various religious groups. Find out what clubs exist in your community by asking teachers, clergy, and recreation leaders.

Some clubs are formed to provide service to others. Many schools have service clubs whose members welcome new students, tutor others who need some help in a certain subject, or serve refreshments at school programs or games. Schools also have clubs relating to subjects taught—such as science, language, reading, math, or specific sports. Other clubs are "honoraries" for outstanding students, such as the National Honor Society. Some clubs encourage hobbies such as hiking, ecology, stamp or coin collecting, photography, cooking, camping, bicycling, and model making.

Most clubs have a purpose or goal. A constitution and by-laws (rules) may be written, explaining the purpose of the club and how the goal is to be reached. The members of most clubs elect officers to lead them. A president leads the meetings. The vice president helps the president and often plans the program of the club. The secretary keeps a written record of what happens in the club so that future members will know what the club has accomplished. Members usually have to pay dues (fees) so that the club can afford any materials that are needed. The treasurer handles all money and keeps a record of it. Most clubs have regular meeting days and special events. These are announced in advance so that members can plan their other activities without having to miss any club meetings.

■ LEARN BY DOING

You could start a club of your own in your school or neighborhood. It might be centered around an activity mentioned in this article or anything else that interests you. ■

ALSO READ: RED CROSS, YOUNG PEOPLE'S ASSOCIATIONS.

COAL Coal is a rock that burns. It is mined from the earth of every continent. It is one of our most important *fuels* (materials that can be burned to get heat). Burning coal provides heat for warming houses and other buildings and for making steam used to power many kinds of machines.

Coal is made up mainly of the element carbon but may also contain water, sulfur, clay, and certain compounds of hydrogen and oxygen, as well as millions of fossils.

Coal was for many years the major industrial fuel, used for railroads, factories, and steamships. Long trainloads of coal cars used to cross the continent, and freighters hauled coals across the seas to satisfy the needs of people everywhere. Today we use electricity, gasoline, diesel fuel, other petroleum products, and even nuclear energy in places in which we once used coal.

Most of the coal mined today was formed hundreds of millions of years ago during two warm, rainy periods called the Coal, or *Carboniferous*, periods. The earlier period lasted about 65 million years, and the other, about 80 million. During these times, shallow seas flooded the continents, making vast swampy areas.

Soft, pulpy trees with green trunks and no bark grew in the swamps. Thick forests of these trees grew rapidly, died, and fell into the water. Being under water kept them from decaying very much. Over hundreds of thousands of years, the partly decayed remains of the trees formed a thick layer of a spongy material called *peat*. Millions of years later, the swamps were covered by layers of clay, sand, or gravel many feet thick. The tremendous weight of this material plus heat from the earth's movement changed the peat to coal.

Kinds of Coal The three main kinds of coal are lignite, bituminous, and anthracite.

Lignite is soft, crumbly, and dark brown. It is also called *brown coal*. It burns with a very smoky flame because it contains much moisture. It does not produce much heat and can burst into flame when in storage. To get rid of much of the moisture, lignite is compressed into bricks. Lignite is mined in North Dakota and Montana.

Bituminous is often called "soft" coal, although it is hard and black. Bituminous coal burns well, but

Lignite

Anthracite

Bituminous

▲ *Three types of coal, with the hardest, anthracite, in the middle.*

◄ *Conditions in early coal mines were very bad. When the men had hacked coal out of the seams, women dragged or carried it through the tunnels.*

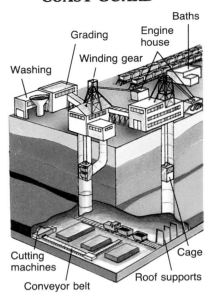

▲ *Inside a modern coal mine. To keep the air fresh inside the mine, giant fans draw fresh air through the tunnels and suck out stale air.*

▼ *Coke is a fuel used in the making of iron and steel. It is made from coal by heating the coal in an oven so that it does not catch fire. Instead it forms coke, coal tar, and coal gas.*

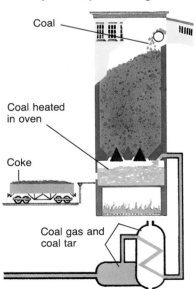

▲ *Below ground, a worker operates a coal-cutting machine.*

with a smoky flame. It is often used in industry because it is cheap. Bituminous goal is mined in the Appalachian Mountains from western Pennsylvania and Ohio through West Virginia, Kentucky, and Tennessee into northern Alabama.

Anthracite is "hard" coal. It is shiny black, has a smooth surface, and breaks with sharp edges. It gives the most heat and burns with very little smoke. It is best for heating houses because it is the cleanest kind of coal. Almost all anthracite mined in the United States comes from Pennsylvania.

Mining Coal Coal is found in the earth in layers, or *seams*. A seam may be a few inches or many feet thick. Around the seams is clay or rock. One way to mine coal is to dig a hole, or shaft, straight down. When the shaft reaches a seam of coal, tunnels are dug sideways into the seam. A shaft usually goes through many seams.

The coal in a seam may be broken up with explosives and then removed by miners using picks and shovels. In modern mines, large machines are used to power huge drills, or augers, that break up the seams, and the coal is put on moving belts that take it to the shaft. This is *shaft* or *underground*

mining. Anthracite coal is mined this way.

In *open pit mining*, or *strip mining*, machines remove the earth above the coal seam. Huge power shovels then break up the seam, scoop up the coal, and empty it into dump trucks or railroad cars to be carried away. Open pit mining can be done only where the coal is close to the surface of the earth. This type of mining is very destructive. It ruins large areas of land, and it can leave many animals homeless.

Coal may be heated in a closed container emptied of air. The coal does not burn, but breaks up into several gases, liquids, and a solid material called *coke*. The gases and coke are used as fuels. The liquids include *benzene* and *coal tar*, from which dyes, medicines, plastics, and hundreds of useful chemical compounds are made.

ALSO READ: EARTH HISTORY, FUEL, MINES AND MINING.

COAST GUARD The Coast Guard is America's police of the coasts. Its job is to make the coasts, rivers, and lakes of the United States safe and to see that ships obey traffic rules. When ships are damaged by collision, fire, or bad weather, the Coast Guard rescues the people and helps save the ships if possible.

The Coast Guard has several hundred ships and boats. Its cruising and patrol *cutters*, which range from about 60 to 400 feet (18 to 120 m) in length, can skim along the water at around 40 miles (65 km) an hour. Among the Coast Guard's other vessels are patrol motorboats, ocean and harbor tugs, fireboats, lightships, and tenders. Many Coast Guard vessels are armed with guns. Seaplanes, helicopters, and other aircraft are also used by the Coast Guard, especially in search and rescue operations. There are about 38,000 active and 23,000 reserve members in the Coast Guard.

The Coast Guard was formed in 1915, but the idea behind it is much older. Special ships of the Revenue Marine patrolled against privateers even during the American Revolution. One of the first cutters was a vessel named *Eagle*. In peacetime, the Coast Guard is part of the U.S. Department of Transportation. The Coast Guard joins the armed forces and becomes part of the U.S. Navy when the country goes to war.

The Coast Guard operates lighthouses and buoys along our seacoasts and on rivers and lakes that are navigable (deep and wide enough for ships). Buoys are anchored to the bottom and are used to mark channels, rocks, and shallow water. Some buoys have flashing lights or clanging bells. Others send radio and radar signals to nearby ships. The Coast Guard's icebreakers are special ships that crunch through solid ice so that other ships can keep moving in winter. To make the waterways as safe as possible, Coast Guard stations all over the country offer free boating safety lessons to everyone.

ALSO READ: BOATS AND BOATING.

COAT OF ARMS A coat of arms is a special sign that identifies a family, a state, or a nation. Armies have carried specially designed banners for thousands of years. Ancient Roman troops were always easy to identify, because at the head of the legion was a special *emblem* (sign) that identified the troops.

But the phrase "coat of arms" comes from the Middle Ages. Soldiers in the 1100's began to paint family emblems on their shields. When closed helmets came to be used, knights were covered from head to toe, and no one could tell friend from enemy. So knights began to wear a loose surcoat (overcoat or cloak) over their armor. Their family

▲ *This motor lifeboat of the U.S. Coast Guard takes part in offshore rescue operations.*

emblem was sewn into the cloth of the surcoat, which made it possible for a man to spot his friends during a battle. People soon began to call this surcoat a "coat of arms," and the name has come to mean any family emblem.

At first, everybody picked whatever coat of arms he liked best. But this soon caused confusion, because many people picked similar designs for their coats of arms. Experts in coats of arms, who were called *heralds*, came into being. Heralds were in charge of picking designs and colors for each family's coat of arms. The work of heralds, called *heraldry*, became quite organized during the 1200's. Armor went out of style in the 1500's because it could not protect a soldier from bullets, which came into wide use at that time. But people liked the idea of having their own family design, so they kept their coats of arms. King Richard III of England set up the Herald's College (College of Arms) in 1484. This college decides which English families can have coats of arms and what the colors and designs will be.

Most countries and states today have coats of arms. They are proudly displayed on official documents and flags.

Before 1915, the Coast Guard was known as the Revenue Cutter Service. The revenue cutter *Harriet Lane* fired the first shot at sea during the Civil War. It stopped a Southern cargo ship from entering the harbor of Charleston, South Carolina, on April 11, 1861.

COAT OF ARMS

SHIELD SHAPES

The shield is the central and most important part of a coat of arms. They come in many shapes that are based on the shields that knights carried for protection.

| vair | or (gold) | argent (silver) | sable (black) | purpure (purple) | gules (red) |

| azure (blue) | vert (green) | ermine |

The tinctures are colors and painted furs that are put on the shield. Two metallic colors (*metals*), five other colors, and two fur designs are commonly used. *Or* (gold) metal is often represented by yellow, and *argent* (silver) is often white. The *ermine* fur looks like white and black ermine tails. The *vair* fur looks like blue and white squirrel skins.

ORDINARIES

| fess | pale | cross | saltire | chief | bend |

The tinctures are put on the shield in bands or geometric shapes called ordinaries. Some of the most common ones are shown here.

DEVICES

Devices are designs that are *charged* or put on the shield. They can be monsters, wild animals, tools, buildings, planets, hands, flowers, and many other things.

A COAT OF ARMS

The shield is only the center of the full coat of arms. It is held up by supporters, *human or animal figures, which stand on a* compartment *or mound of grass. The helm is surmounted by a* crest. *Underneath the shield, on the compartment, is a* motto. *These are the heraldic arms of Zambia, which also appear on the presidential flag of that nation.*

ONE ZAMBIA ONE NATION

■ **LEARN BY DOING**

Study the illustration and design your own coat of arms. First, draw a shield in any shape you want and pick two or three *tinctures* to put on it. Divide up the face of the shield, adding *ordinaries*. Think of *devices* (designs) to put on the shield. Is your family associated with a certain animal, flower or trade? Surround your shield with *supporters* (figures or animals) and *mantling* (or bands of feathers). Finally, invent a short *motto* and write it on a ribbon band under the shield. ■

ALSO READ: ARMOR, KNIGHTHOOD, NOBILITY.

COCHISE (about 1815–1874)

Cochise was a leader of the Chiricahua Apache Indians. For hundreds of years this small tribe roamed the mountains along the border between Arizona and Mexico.

In 1861 an inexperienced U.S. Army lieutenant arrested Cochise and three other Apache chiefs for a crime they had not committed. Cochise cut his way through a tent and escaped. In return, the soldiers killed Cochise's brother and sons, and the three other chiefs were hanged.

Other Apaches rallied behind Cochise, who led them in a war against the white settlers. They attacked white settlements, tortured and killed people, and burned towns throughout the Southwest. Cochise became known for this brilliant military strategy. With only 200 warriors, he defeated U.S. Army troops again and again. The Apaches often rode for hours without rest to escape the Army. In 1872, Cochise agreed to a peace treaty when his tribe was promised a reservation. After Cochise died, the government broke its promise and moved the tribe off the land.

ALSO READ: APACHE INDIANS; INDIANS, AMERICAN; INDIAN WARS.

CODES AND CIPHERS

CODES AND CIPHERS Codes and ciphers have been used for hundreds of years to transmit secret information. In a code, each word is changed. In a cipher, each letter of each word is disguised.

It is thought that the Egyptians used some codes in writing messages in hieroglyphics. Codes are mentioned in the Bible. The simple code in which one letter of the alphabet is used in place of another letter was probably first used in the time of the Roman emperor Julius Caesar, who also sent messages in cipher.

Both the British and the Americans used codes in the American Revolution. During World War II, the United States code experts "broke" (figured out) the complicated cipher that the Japanese were using. U.S. forces were able to find out enemy plans and military movements for months, until the Japanese realized what had happened.

Francis Bacon, an English philosopher, invented in 1605 a cipher in which the letters *a* and *b*, in five-letter combinations, stood for each letter in the alphabet. This proved that a cipher using only two different signs could be used to send information.

■ LEARN BY DOING

One day in school, Jerry gave Arthur a message in a secret code. It said: EMOC OT EHT ESUOHEERT THGINOT TA NEVES. POT TERCES. It was signed: YRREJ. Arthur knew that "YRREJ" meant Jerry, so he could easily *decode* (change to regular language) the rest of the secret message. Can you?

Jerry used a very simple code for his message. He just wrote each word backwards. This is one kind of *transposition code*. In a transposition code, the same letters are used as in the original message, but they are transposed, or rearranged.

Here is Jerry's message written in a

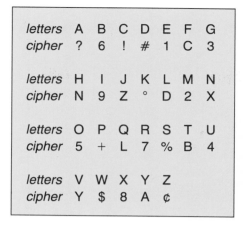

letters	A	B	C	D	E	F	G
cipher	?	6	!	#	1	C	3

letters	H	I	J	K	L	M	N
cipher	N	9	Z	°	D	2	X

letters	O	P	Q	R	S	T	U
cipher	5	+	L	7	%	B	4

letters	V	W	X	Y	Z
cipher	Y	$	8	A	¢

more complicated cipher. !521 B5 BN1 B711N54%1 ?B %1Y1X B5+%1!71B.

The message here is written in a *substitution cipher*. Symbols are substituted for the letters in the original message, but the letters are left in the same order. Letters, numbers, or any other symbols (even ones you make up) can be used in a substitution cipher. Above is the "alphabet" of symbols that was used to encipher the message above.

Try making up a code of your own. One way to have a very, very secret code would be to use both substitution *and* transposition. First substitute a symbol for each letter, and then rearrange the letters. ■

CODY, WILLIAM F. see BUFFALO BILL.

COELENTERATE Jellyfish, sea fans, corals, and hydroids all look a little like strange undersea plants. But don't be fooled—they are animals that belong to *phylum* Coelenterata. There are about 10,000 kinds. Most of them live in salt water, but some—called *hydras*—are common in unpolluted fresh water.

It is often hard to recognize coelenterates as animals. A jellyfish washed onto a beach seems to be a shapeless lump. Corals in a tropical underwater "garden" look like

▲ *Cochise, great warrior leader of the Chiricahua Apache Indians.*

▼ *Sea anemones are single polyps. They do not form colonies. Their brightly colored tentacles look like delicate flower petals. But they are quite deadly to the small creatures on which the polyps feed.*

▲ *The dahlia anemone is common in rock pools quite high on the shore. When uncovered by the tide, the animal pulls its tentacles right inside its body and contracts to a blob of jelly.*

strange plants or rocks. Sea anemones resemble flowers. All of these coelenterates, however, are actually soft-bodied animals, classed among the lower forms of the animal kingdom.

Coelenterates come in hundreds of different sizes and shapes, but they are all alike in certain ways. Their main body part is always a hollow tube that digests food, like an intestine. An opening at the end of the tube acts like a mouth. All coelenterates have stinging cells that paralyze fish or other animals. Coelenterates are not only animals, but *carnivores* (meat eaters). Tentacles with sting cells stun the prey and pull it into the awaiting mouth. Digestive juices break it down into a kind of broth. Small coelenterates live on plankton, which are tiny forms of sea life. Larger coelenterates, such as the bigger jellyfish, trap and eat fish.

Polyps and Medusas Coelenterates spend their lives either as *polyps* or *medusas*. Polyps are attached, or rooted, to a surface. Medusas are free-swimming.

A polyp is a simple little animal. It has a fleshy stalk or intestine, a mouth, reproductive organs, and moving tentacles. It grows from some base such as rock, the ocean floor, or even seaweed, and waits for prey to touch its stinging tentacles. One marine polyp, the sea anemone, can move itself around by creeping. It may measure several inches across the top. It does not live in a colony.

Most polyps do live in colonies. Coral growths are made up of many polyps living together. They form a limestone skeleton around themselves. The colorful sea fans of tropical waters are colonies of polyps with a horny internal skeleton. Plankton is washed through the fan by water currents and is trapped by the polyps. Sea whips and hydroids (sea plumes) live in colonies.

Medusas are coelenterates that actively swim through the water or float

▲ *The flowerlike shapes in a living coral colony are made up of thousands of individual polyps, each only 0.4 inches (10 mm) in diameter.*

▼ *A jellyfish trails its long, stinging tentacles. It can fire the stinging cells on its tentacles into its prey like tiny harpoons.*

on the surface. They are commonly called jellyfish. There are many hundreds of shapes, sizes, and types of medusas. Some are fairly good swimmers, moving with jerks of their jelly-like bodies. Others have bells, or air-filled sacs, to keep them afloat. Like polyps, they have flowing tentacles to trap their prey. Medusas usually reproduce by scattering eggs in the water.

Some interesting coelenterates spend part of their lives as polyps and part as medusas. Hydroids, or sea plumes, are an example. As polyps they always form large colonies, which look like feathery plants growing in the water. Individual polyps line the stems and branches. The polyps produce small medusas that split away from the sea plume and swim like tiny jellyfish. They produce eggs and sperm. The fertilized eggs turn into tiny *larvae*, which settle on a firm surface and turn into polyps that begin a new colony.

ALSO READ: ANIMAL KINGDOM, CORAL, JELLYFISH, MARINE LIFE.

COFFEE Coffee is the most popular drink among adults in many parts of the world. People probably first learned to use coffee as a beverage in Abyssinia (Ethiopia) about 1,300 years ago. By the A.D. 800's, people of Arabia learned to make a usable beverage out of raw coffee. Later the use of coffee spread to Persia and Turkey. It reached Europe and America in the 1500's and 1600's. Coffee plantations were begun in Indonesia in 1800 and in South America in 1840. South America is the world's top coffee producer, but Africa's output is increasing each year.

Coffee comes from an evergreen tree that can grow 15 to 40 feet (4.5 to 12 m) tall, but the trees are kept trimmed to only 6 or 9 feet (2 or 3 m) so that their fruit can be reached more easily. The trees bear red berries called "cherries," which contain two seeds or beans enclosed in yellow pulp and surrounded by a tough skin. Coffee growers remove the skin and pulp, and dry the beans in the sun.

The dried beans are shipped to coffee roasting plants in many countries, where different beans are blended (mixed). Each year, about 3 billion pounds (1.4 billion kg) come to the United States. The beans are roasted at 900°F (480°C) for 16 minutes. Later, the roasted beans are ground into powder.

When ground coffee is soaked in boiling water, certain substances in the powder dissolve in the water. This process, called *brewing*, is the way we make the coffee we drink. The undissolved part of the coffee, the *grounds*, is thrown away.

Large quantities of coffee may be brewed in a factory. Then the water is boiled away and the brown substance that remains is again ground to a powder. This powder is *instant coffee*. Instant coffee is ready to drink as soon as hot water is added. *Freeze-dried coffee* is brewed, instantly frozen into crystals, and dehydrated (water removed).

Coffee contains a substance called *caffeine*, which can make you temporarily excited and keep you from sleeping well. *Decaffeinated* coffee has had the caffeine removed.

ALSO READ: SOUTH AMERICA.

COHAN, GEORGE M. (1878–1942) George M. Cohan's parents were theatrical performers who once carried their baby on stage in a play. This was the beginning of George's long career in musical theater.

George was born in Providence, Rhode Island. He became a regular vaudeville performer at the age of nine, when he joined his family's act, the Four Cohans. He danced, sang, and acted in short, funny plays.

He began writing plays and songs as a young man. His musical comedy *Little Johnny Jones* contained the hit song "Give My Regards to Broadway," which made Cohan a success. He wrote about 50 shows and many famous songs, including "It's a Grand Old Flag," and "I'm a Yankee Doodle Dandy." Cohan himself starred in most of his productions.

Cohan made musical comedy very popular because he was able to use songs and jokes to show the optimistic, happy feelings that many Americans held at the time. His song "Over There" was the hit of World War I. In 1940, Congress awarded him a gold medal for this song as well as for his other contributions to American musical theater. The movie *Yankee Doodle Dandy* is based on his life.

ALSO READ: MUSICAL COMEDY, VAUDEVILLE.

▲ *Coffee flowers and "cherries," each of which (enlarged) contains two seeds, or coffee beans.*

"Mocha" is sometimes used as another word for coffee. The name comes from Mocha in Yemen, because almost all the world's coffee supply passed through that port in the 1600's. Today, "mocha" also means coffee flavored with chocolate.

▼ *George M. Cohan, American actor, playwright, and songwriter.*

▲ *A Greek coin, of an unusual oval shape, minted about 400 B.C. It is decorated with a picture of a graceful horse. Coins are often collected because they are fine works of art.*

▲ *A coin of ancient Rome showing the face of Jupiter, king of the gods in Roman mythology. Many coins honor national leaders and heroes.*

▶ *A Scottish twenty-pound piece from the reign of James VI. Only 18 specimens are known to exist.*

▲ *A twenty-dollar United States gold piece. The United States stopped minting gold coins regularly in 1933, though in 1986 American Eagle gold coins were specially minted.*

COINS Have a look at the coins in your purse or your pocket. You will probably find four different values—quarter, dime, nickel, and penny. What might you do with these coins? Put them into a piggy bank? Exchange them for some candy, ice cream, or a ride on a bus? We call coins, and the paper money that goes with them, a means of exchange—in other words, you can use them to buy something.

Before coins were invented about 3,000 years ago, people had to barter (trade) something they had for whatever they wanted. Barter is not always convenient. If you have potatoes to exchange, but the baker wants a pair of shoes, you cannot get bread. So people began to use coins as tokens of value. For a long time coins were made of *precious metals*, particularly gold and silver, which have a value as metal. Later people realized that any metal would do as long as everybody agreed that each coin was a token for a certain value.

▲ *An ancient Greek coin with the head of Apollo.*

Making coins is called *minting*. U.S. coins are made at mints in Denver, Philadelphia, and San Francisco. The coins are stamped out of long strips of metal. From time to time the mint issues coins to commemorate important events. One of these was issued to commemorate the restoration of the Statue of Liberty in 1986.

■ **LEARN BY DOING**

If you want to study coins more, you could form a small collection. Begin by choosing one coin of each value and putting it in a special album. If you hunt through your change you may find older coins with different designs on them. You may also find some coins from other countries to add to your collection. ■

ALSO READ: DOLLAR, MONEY.

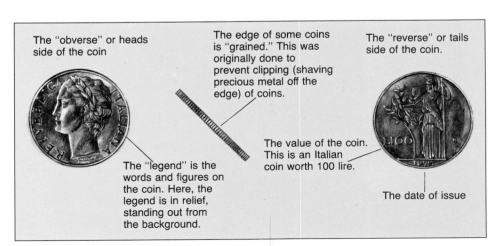

The "obverse" or heads side of the coin

The edge of some coins is "grained." This was originally done to prevent clipping (shaving precious metal off the edge) of coins.

The "reverse" or tails side of the coin.

The "legend" is the words and figures on the coin. Here, the legend is in relief, standing out from the background.

The value of the coin. This is an Italian coin worth 100 lire.

The date of issue

COLLECTING In any home there are things that someday may be valuable. A book, poster, or dish that has little value now may be worth much money in years to come. What do you think you may save that will be valuable when you are old? Most collections are of items once used for everyday living. Scarves, hats, dishes, spoons, antique furniture, tools, or charms for a bracelet are examples of such collections. So are books and paintings.

But hobby collections are not necessarily to be used. They are mainly for pleasure, study, and display. Some collections, such as stamps, coins, and autographs, can be very valuable. In 1980, a collector bought one of the world's rarest postage stamps, the British Guiana 1856 one-cent, for $850,000.

Collections can be more than just fun. A collection can be a "history book" in today's fast-changing world. Some hobbyists have collections that may seem strange. There are people who are interested in the American West, for example, who collect barbed wire. Pieces of the 400 varieties are sold at auction for as much as four or five dollars. This may sound peculiar, but a collector can sometimes tell a lot about the history of an area just by knowing which type of barbed wire was used.

Not all collections are valuable. Many collectors travel and save mementos of their trips. They ask for menus or placemats from restaurants, and drinking straws, toothpicks, and matchbooks are also popular *collectibles*. Hobbyists often save things that are found near their own homes. Nature collections are fascinating. Collecting small pieces of rocks and minerals can make a hike in the woods very exciting.

Some collections, such as rare stamps, cost money. Other kinds, such as leaf collections, are absolutely free. With more than 1,000 different

▲ *A collection of decorative antiques. The buying and selling of such collectibles can involve huge sums of money.*

kinds of trees to collect from, people in the cities, suburbs, and the country can have a fine collection of leaves in no time at all. Trees also provide fine wood collections. Look for small branches about 2 inches (5 cm) in diameter lying around on the ground. These can be cut through the center so that the wood grain shows. After you sand them smooth, you can apply a layer of shellac to make them shiny and to bring out the beauty of the wood grain.

Collections have little meaning if they are just tossed into a box or a dresser drawer. They become a hobby only when they have developed a meaning and purpose. Collections must be properly organized, cared for, and displayed. They should also be *annotated*—that is, furnished with explanatory notes that tell where the item was found, its age, and any other interesting information. Many kinds of collections tell a story from an early time until the present. Nature collections can tell the story of a certain area. A collector from a fishing community might keep fishhooks or nets. Seashell collections are beautiful, and the shells can tell a fascinating story about the animals who lived in them. Fossils are often collected in areas where many are found. Young

▼ *A stamp collection could include as many U.S. postage stamps with pictures of Presidents as you could find.*

▲ *Designing and operating model railroad layouts is a fascinating hobby for enthusiasts of all ages.*

▼ *A collection of French playing cards. The two tarot cards on the left date from the 1400's; the two on the right from the 1600's.*

Things to collect can be found in all kinds of places. Most people begin with objects found near their homes or among their friends. A stamp collection can begin with letters and postcards from vacationing friends. Baseball cards are popular as collections among young ball players. Buttons can be found in old button boxes or jars in grandmother's attic. Autographs can be exchanged with friends and relatives. Many famous people will send their autographs if you ask them to do so. Send a three-by-five-inch file card for the person to sign, and include a self-addressed stamped envelope.

people who have grandmothers with attics full of interesting old things can collect antiques. People who live near a racetrack can collect horseshoes. Many people like to save old automobile license plates, although some plates are expensive.

People in many parts of the country collect Indian arrowheads, tools, and bits of pottery that they find on hikes through the forests. Button collecting has great historical value and interest. Buttons tell much about the changing fashions in clothing and industry. Bottles can also make an interesting collection. Badges or insignia are fun to collect.

Hobbyists who collect things are sometimes given special names. Stamp collectors are called *philatelists*. Coin collectors are known as *numismatists*. Rock collectors are often called *rock hounds*, and those who collect matchbooks are *phillumenists*.

Collectors follow certain rules about the care which must be given to each article. Study books and manuals to make sure your collection is being kept properly. In nature collections, it is important to make notes about the specimen—rock, piece of wood, or leaf—at the time it is gathered. Label the specimen at once with a number written on adhesive tape or gummed paper. Note where it was found, when, and its condition. Specimens can often be carried home in a protective plastic bag. Once home, put your notes neatly on index cards and put the cards in a file.

Collections can be displayed in many interesting ways. A wood collection can be displayed by hanging the specimens with a screw eye and hook from the bottom of a wall shelf. Leaf collections are often kept in a scrapbook, where each leaf is protected by a plastic "window." The most beautiful leaves can be hung on the wall by mounting them behind glass in inexpensive picture frames.

There is no end to ways in which your collection can be displayed. You can often get ideas from other people who have the same type of collection.

For further information on:
Background, *see* HOBBIES.
Man-made Objects to Collect, *see* ANTIQUE, AUTOGRAPH, BOOK, BUT-

TON, CLOCKS AND WATCHES, DOLL, FURNITURE, GLASS, JEWELRY, POTTERY AND CHINA, RECORDING, STAMP COLLECTING, TOYS.

Things from Nature to Collect, *see* BARK, BUTTERFLIES AND MOTHS, FLOWER, FOSSIL, LEAF, ROCK, SHELL, TROPICAL FISH, WOOD.

Do-It-Yourself Collection Hobbies, *see* CARVING, DRAWING, ENAMELING, MODEL MAKING, PAINTING, PHOTOGRAPHY, SCULPTURE, SEWING.

COLLEGES AND UNIVERSITIES

Many young people decide to follow careers that require more training than they have had in high school. After graduation, some will go on to technical institutes, business schools, or other institutions for learning special skills. Still others will continue their education at one of the more than 3,000 colleges, universities, professional schools, teachers' colleges, junior or community colleges, or at one of the military academies in the United States.

These *institutions of higher learning,* as they are often called, grew out of the universities and colleges that developed in Europe hundreds of years ago. The ancient Romans called a group of people working together for a common purpose a *universitas.* An organization to increase learning became known as a university.

Early History The first European university was founded at Salerno, Italy, about A.D. 850. It became famous as a medical school. In 1088 the University of Bologna was established as a student organization for protection against merchants and others who had raised prices of food and housing. The students hired their teachers and ran the school, which became famous for its legal scholars. The University of Paris was, however, organized and run by the teachers, who charged fees to their students. Universities later were con-

trolled by *administrators* who set policies for both the *faculties* (teachers) and the students. In the 1200's, students at Oxford and Cambridge universities in England formed separate "colleges" within their universities. All the students studying one subject lived, ate, and worked together in one college. Today, the word "college" has two meanings in the United States. It can mean an institution of higher learning or an undergraduate division or school within a university.

Higher Education in the U.S. Harvard University in Cambridge, Massachusetts, is the oldest institution of higher learning in the United States. It was founded as a college in 1636 to prepare young men to be ministers. Many other American colleges were also started by religious groups in order to train young people as leaders in their faith. But as time went by, special colleges called *theological seminaries* were established to train ministers. Other colleges were founded to educate young people in more general subjects. These later became known as *liberal arts colleges.* By 1800, there were 26 U.S. colleges. By the Civil War, 182 were operating.

> The first college in the United States was Harvard, founded at Cambridge, Massachusetts, in 1636. This was followed by William and Mary, Williamsburg, Virginia (1693); Yale, New Haven, Connecticut (1701); Princeton, New Jersey (1746); and Columbia, New York City (1754). All these are now universities except for William and Mary.

SOME FAMOUS OLD COLLEGES AND UNIVERSITIES

University/College	Country	Year it began
1. Han Lin	China	200
2. Salerno	Italy	850
3. Karweein, Fez	Morocco	859
4. Al-Azhar, Cairo	Egypt	950
5. Bologna	Italy	1088
6. Paris	France	1150
7. Oxford	England	1167
8. Cambridge	England	1209
9. Prague	Czechoslovakia	1347
10. Vienna	Austria	1364
11. Heidelberg	Germany	1385
12. St. Andrews	Scotland	1411
13. Mexico, Mexico City	Mexico	1551
14. Trinity, Dublin	Ireland	1591
15. Harvard, Cambridge, Mass.	U.S.	1636
16. William and Mary, Williamsburg, Virginia	U.S.	1693
17. Yale, New Haven, Conn.	U.S.	1701
18. Princeton, New Jersey	U.S.	1746
19. Moscow	U.S.S.R.	1755
20. McGill, Montreal	Canada	1821

Several professional schools offered courses in such fields as engineering, agriculture, and applied science. *Normal schools* prepared people to be teachers. Such schools are now called teachers' colleges.

Johns Hopkins University was founded in Baltimore, Maryland, in 1876. It was the first university in the United States to have the characteristics of the university as we know it today, and it set a new pattern for American higher education.

For hundreds of years, only young men went to college. It was not until 1825 that a college education was offered to women in the U.S. At first, they had to attend separate schools, but Oberlin College in Ohio had both men and women students in 1832. It was the first *coeducational* institution. Some schools still have only men or only women students, but most schools are now coeducational.

Congress passed an important bill called the Land-Grant College Act in 1862. It granted each state 30,000 acres (12,000 hectares) of land for each senator and congressman representing that state in Congress. The money from the sale of this land was to help support at least one college whose main purpose was to train students in agriculture and "the mechanic arts," but not to exclude "other scientific studies." Twenty-eight states founded "A and M" (agricultural and mechanical) colleges. Many of these schools have become important centers for training engineers and scientists.

Modern Colleges in the U.S. Colleges and universities both offer education beyond high school, but there are some important differences. First of all, two-year colleges (called *junior colleges* or *community colleges*) award a special certificate called an *associate's degree* to their graduates. Some students begin work after earning an associate's degree. Others go on to study at a four-year college or university. These students receive an undergraduate or *bachelor's degree* after four years of study. Usually, this is the only degree offered by liberal arts colleges.

Universities are generally larger institutions than colleges, and they offer programs in many different fields, such as home economics, business administration, or education, as well as liberal arts (courses such as language, music, art, and the social sciences). Within a university, each field of study is called a School or College—such as the School of Engineering or the College of Education. Universities also offer graduate studies that lead to a *master's degree*, and then to a *doctor's degree* in a special profession such as medicine, dentistry, law, education, or divinity. Many universities offer courses for study and research beyond the doctor's degree. Some have extension divisions, which give courses to part-time students and those who are not working toward any degree.

Private and Public There are two general kinds of colleges and universities—private and public. More than half of the privately sponsored liberal arts colleges are, or have been, controlled by or connected with a church. Private universities usually have no

▼ *The Wren building, part of the campus of the College of William and Mary, was built in colonial times.*

connections with church or religious groups. They depend on students' payments, and on grants (gifts) from wealthy people and large businesses. Public universities are supported by the federal and state governments. Public colleges (junior or community colleges) are most often supported by local governments. The Military Academy, Naval Academy, Air Force Academy, and Coast Guard Academy are all supported by the Federal Government.

The Federal Government also sometimes provides financial loans to students and grants to veterans of military service. The GI bill passed in 1944 paid the education and living costs of millions of servicemen and women returning from World War II, so they could receive higher education.

Many students get financial help by winning scholarships, which pay part or all of the cost of going to college. Others "work their way through college" by taking jobs on or near the campus. Students can also arrange for loans of money that they agree to pay back after graduation.

ALSO READ: EDUCATION, SCHOOL, U.S. SERVICE ACADEMIES.

COLLINS, MICHAEL (born 1930) While Neil Armstrong and Edwin "Buzz" Aldrin made history by landing on the moon, a third man waited for them in a spacecraft orbiting the moon. He was Michael Collins, the Apollo 11 command module pilot. His job was to guide the big spacecraft to the moon and back again to Earth. Collins practiced more than 800 hours for his part in the mission.

Michael Collins was born in Rome, Italy. His father was a military expert assigned to the United States embassy there. Collins graduated from the U.S. Military Academy at West Point in 1952 and became a jet test pilot for the Air Force. In 1963 he was chosen

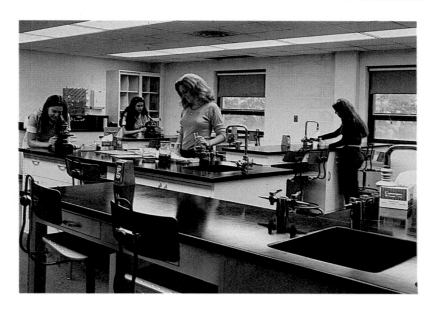

to be an astronaut. Collins "walked" in space for more than 27 minutes during the Gemini 10 mission in July 1966. Three years later he piloted the historic Apollo 11 flight to the moon.

Collins left the space program in January 1970. He is director of the Smithsonian Institution's Aviation and Space Museum, where historic airplanes and spaceflight equipment and photographs are displayed and stored.

ALSO READ: ALDRIN, EDWIN; ARMSTRONG, NEIL; ASTRONAUT; MOON; SPACE TRAVEL.

COLOMBIA Colombia is a republic in South America. It is about as large as Texas, New Mexico, and Oklahoma combined. It has a coastline on two oceans—the Pacific and the Caribbean waters of the Atlantic. (See the map with the article on SOUTH AMERICA.) The capital and largest city of Colombia is Bogotá, 9,000 feet (2,700 m) high in fog-shrouded mountains. It is a center of art, learning, business, and government, proud of being a city with customs and speech like those of Spain. Colombia's main seaport is Cartagena, where the Royal Spanish Fleet gathered in olden times. Both

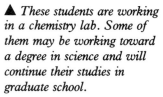

▲ *These students are working in a chemistry lab. Some of them may be working toward a degree in science and will continue their studies in graduate school.*

▲ *Michael Collins, command module pilot for the flight of Apollo 11.*

COLOMBIA

Capital City: Bogotá (3,960,000 people).
Area: 439,769 square miles (1,138,914 sq. km).
Population: 31,820,000.
Government: Republic.
Natural Resources: Coal, copper, gold, oil, precious stones, silver.
Export Products: Coffee, bananas, flowers, sugar, textiles and clothes.
Unit of Money: Peso.
Official Language: Spanish.

Colombia produces more coffee than any other South American country except Brazil. It comes third to Brazil and Chile in gold mining. Colombia produces nearly all the world's emeralds.

▼ *Bogotá is the capital and largest city of Colombia. It lies in a basin in the Andes Mountains.*

Bogotá and Cartagena were founded in the 1500's by Spanish colonists.

Colombia has a varied climate and a varied terrain. Much of the land is a hot, damp jungle. Few people live in the jungle because it is uncomfortable and unhealthy. Grassy plains stretch across the eastern part of Colombia, and swampy lowlands are found along the coast. Northwestern Colombia has cool mountain areas. People come from many countries to ski in the mountain snow practically at the equator. Most of Colombia's people live in the northwest, where the highlands are very fertile. Coffee trees, with their shiny, dark green leaves and red-orange berries, cover the mountainsides and valleys. Coffee is Colombia's most important crop. The highland Colombian coffee is famous throughout the world.

An underground church carved into a giant cave with walls of glistening white salt—that sounds like something from a fairy tale. But in Colombia there is such a church, called the Salt Cathedral, 345 feet (105 m) beneath the surface of the Earth. It is big enough to hold 10,000 people at one time. Visitors from all over the world come to Colombia to see the Salt Cathedral. They also visit nearby salt mines, which have been in use for hundreds of years.

Only Indians lived in Colombia for many thousands of years. The Spaniards conquered Colombia in the

1500's. They made it the center of a Spanish colony called New Granada (Granada is a province of Spain). Most of the Colombian people today are *mestizos*, people who are part Indian and part Spanish. The Colombians won their independence from Spain in 1819, under the leadership of the great Venezuelan general, Simon Bolívar. The Isthmus of Panama was part of Colombia from Spanish colonial days. The Panamanians revolted several times in the late 1800's. With U.S. help, they broke away in 1903. Today, Colombia is a democratic republic but has many social and economic problems.

ALSO READ: BOLÍVAR, SIMON; PANAMA; SOUTH AMERICA; SPANISH HISTORY.

COLONIAL LIFE see AMERICAN COLONIES.

COLONY A colony is a settlement in a new territory founded by people from another country. People who found a colony are called *colonists*. The country the colonists come from is called the *mother country*. It is often far away from the colony. But no matter how far away the mother country is, many colonists feel loyal to it. They often speak the mother country's language. They are ruled by the same government. They sell their goods to merchants in the mother country. A colony is a possession, or territory, belonging to the mother country, not an independent nation.

When settlers move into new territory and start a colony, the people who originally lived in the area often lose their independence and are subjected to foreign rule. Spanish soldiers, for example, had to fight bloody battles, usually resulting in massacres, with many Indian tribes in order to take over the lands of South and Central America. And colonists killed many North American Indians and drove many others out of their homes in order to found colonies. In almost every case, when a colony is started, it is done at the expense of the earlier inhabitants.

Some of the earliest colonies were those established by the ancient Greeks and Romans in lands around the Mediterranean Sea. During the 1500's and 1600's, many people from Europe founded colonies in America. Most of the colonies in North America were founded by people from England. Quebec, in Canada, was founded by French colonists. The nations of South America began as colonies founded by people from Spain and Portugal. Other nations that began as colonies are Australia and New Zealand. These two countries were British colonies. In time, many of these colonies wanted to become independent of their mother countries. The 13 colonies of North America became the United States after they won their independence in the American Revolution.

The powerful nations of Europe founded *nonsettlement colonies* in Africa and Asia in the 1800's. People from Europe did not go to these colonies just to live. The Europeans sent just enough soldiers, officials, and businessmen to rule the people who already lived there. Sometimes the inhabitants were forced to be slaves. These nonsettlement colonies were important as markets and as sources

of raw materials for factories in the ruling countries. Many nonsettlement colonies became independent after World War II. Some, such as Algeria and Indonesia, had to fight bitter wars to become independent. Others, such as the Philippines, were given their independence without a war. One of the most famous remaining British colonies is Hong Kong, a city bordering Communist China. The land on which much of Hong Kong is built was leased from China in 1898 and is due to revert to China in 1997.

International economic and military cooperation have made the establishment of new colonies, or *colonialism*, unnecessary and almost nonexistent today.

ALSO READ: AMERICAN COLONIES, COMMONWEALTH OF NATIONS, SOUTH AMERICA, UNITED NATIONS. *For individual countries see Index.*

COLOR   Light is made up of colors. Wherever light exists, color does, too. When there is no light, you "see" black. Black is the absence of light. It is not a color at all. You can see from the pictures that a tree that is green in light appears black at night, and that a shadow is black because a solid object blocks out the light.

■ LEARN BY DOING

The colors that make up white light are called the *spectrum*. The main colors of the spectrum are red, orange,

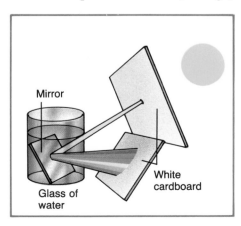

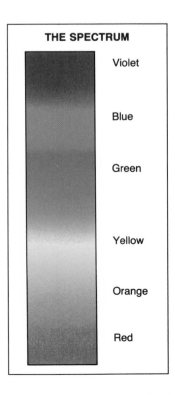

THE SPECTRUM

Violet

Blue

Green

Yellow

Orange

Red

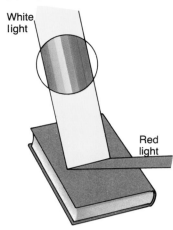

▲ *An object is red because it reflects only red light.*

▲ *White light viewed through a finely woven cloth will show the spectrum as a colorful pattern.*

yellow, green, blue, indigo, and violet. You can make a spectrum of light colors by using water to form a *prism*. Put a small mirror in a glass of water so that it forms an angle as shown in the drawing on page 599. When sunlight hits the mirror, the short waves of violet are bent more than the other colors. Red is bent the least; the other colors fall in between. ■

Colors look different from each other because light moves much as waves do, and each color of light has a different *wavelength*. The wavelength is what makes red light different from waves of any other color. Light waves are very short. About 36,000 red waves cover only an inch (2.5 cm)! Violet has the shortest visible wavelength, and red has the longest. A single color is spread over a small band of wavelengths that cannot be separated by a prism.

You can easily see another type of color spectrum by looking at a white light through a silk scarf or any finely woven material, such as a handkerchief. The colors are brightest if you look at a small bright light at night or in a darkened room. The colorful pattern you see shows that light rays behave as waves, very much like ocean waves or sound waves. Sound waves go around corners, down halls, and through doors. Ocean waves work around rocks and piers. Light

▲ *Light may be broken up into a diffraction pattern of many colors when it is reflected on a polished metal surface on which several equally spaced lines have been cut.*

waves curve around tiny objects, such as the fine scarf threads. Red light goes farther around solid objects than all the other colors because its wavelength is the longest. These different wavelengths of colors cause white light to break into spectacular *diffraction patterns* as the light passes tiny objects. You can see these lovely patterns in soap bubbles, raindrops, and oil slicks.

Kinds of Colors Some people can see almost 100 colors in the spectrum. However, white light, and indeed any other color can be made by mixing different amounts of only three col-

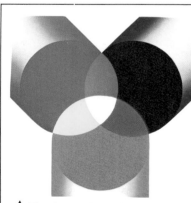

▲ The three primary light colors are red, green, and blue. Other colors are made by mixing them.

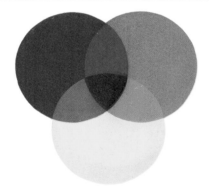

▲ Mixing paints is different from mixing lights. You cannot make white by mixing colored paints.

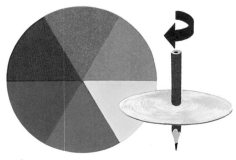

▲ White light is made up of a mixture of colors. You can see this if you spin a colored top—the colors merge into white.

ors. These are called *primary* colors. Red, green, and blue light form a group of primary colors. The colors in color television are made from different mixtures of these three colors. The color wheel for rays of light is shown in the picture.

Secondary colors are those made by mixing two primary colors together. These can be seen in the illustration—turquoise (blue-green), yellow, and magenta (purple-red). Yellow, for example, is made by mixing green and red primary colors of light. *Complementary* colors make white lights when two are mixed. One of them must be primary and the other a secondary color. Blue and yellow are complementary colors. You can mix your own colored rays of light by shining flashlights through different colors of cellophane to make many beautiful colors of light.

A *pigment* is the substance that gives an object its color. Grass, apples, hair, and paint, for example, are all pigmented. Transparent things, such as glass or water, have no pigment in them, so they are called "colorless." The color of pigmented objects is named for the color that people see. Red paint soaks up or *absorbs* all of the colors in white light except red. Red paint bounces back, or *reflects* red, which is then the only visible color.

The primary colors of pigments are turquoise (blue-green), yellow, and magenta (purple-red). On the color wheel for pigments, or paint colors, complementary colors are opposite each other. If you could carefully mix the pure primary colors, you would see black. Any color of paint can be made from the primary colors. Colors are lightened to *tints* by adding white paint. Dark colors are made by adding black paint or paint of a complementary color.

ALSO READ: COLOR BLINDNESS, KALEI-DOSCOPE, LIGHT, RAINBOW, SPECTRUM.

COLORADO The name "Colorado" is a Spanish word meaning "red." Early Spanish explorers found reddish rock along a river that they discovered, so they named the river *Colorado*. The name was given—much later—to the state where the river begins.

The Land It is easy to draw a map of Colorado because the state is a rectangle. The northern and southern boundaries are straight lines that run from west to east. The western and eastern boundaries are straight, too. They run from north to south.

Draw a vertical (north-south) line that divides your map of Colorado into two parts. Draw this line a little to the right (east) of the middle of the state. The dividing line is what we call "105 degrees west longitude," called the "105th meridian" for short. (Meridians of longitude are reference lines that run from the North Pole to the South Pole on globes and maps.)

The Rocky Mountains cover the state west of the meridian. This part of Colorado is high. The High Plains lie east of the dividing line. They *are* high, but still much lower than the mountains. The High Plains are a section of the Great Plains that cross the United States from north to south. But they are hillier than most of the Great Plains.

The two parts of Colorado—west-

One of Colorado's nicknames is "Centennial State" because it joined the Union in 1876—just 100 years after the signing of the Declaration of Independence.

▼ *Monument Valley is part of the Colorado Plateau. The towers, columns and castle-like masses of rock are completely natural monuments.*

▲ *Giant sandstone formations reach into the sky in the Garden of the Gods near Colorado Springs.*

Colorado is the highest state in the Union. Its average height is 6,800 feet (2,073 m) above sea level. The state has more than half of the highest peaks in the United States.

ern and eastern—slope in different directions. They do this because the ridge of the Rocky Mountains runs through the state. The Great Divide, also named the *Continental Divide*, is near the 105th meridian. If you remember that rivers flow downhill, you can look at Colorado's rivers to learn the slope of the land.

One long river, the Colorado, flows through the mountainous part of the state. It is on the western side of the Great Divide. The Colorado flows westward, so we know that the land slopes down to the west.

The Arkansas and South Platte rivers are east of the Great Divide. They flow eastward, showing that the land slopes that way. The High Plains are about one mile (1.6 km) above the level of the sea at the base of the Rockies. Near the border of Nebraska and Kansas, on the eastern edge of the state, they are two-thirds of a mile (1.2 km) above sea level.

You can see both parts of Colorado from Denver, the state capital. Denver, often called the "mile-high city," is on the 105th meridian. The jagged wall of the Rockies is west of the city. Some nearby mountains are so high that they have snow even in summer. East of Denver are the hills of the High Plains.

Climate The state's climate is generally dry and sunny. However, because of differences in altitude, there can be extreme temperature differences within short distances. For instance, in winter, the average temperature is about 29°F (−2°C) on the plains and about 11°F (−12°C) in the mountains. In summer, the average temperature is about 70°F (21°C) on the plains and about 55°F (13°C) in the mountains. Colorado's highest temperature, 118°F (48°C) was recorded at Bennett on July 11, 1888. Its lowest occurred at Taylor Park Dam on Feb. 1, 1951: 60°F below zero (−51°C).

Differences in precipitation are great, too. The High Plains have the state's good farmland. But too little rain falls for most crops. Winter snow piles up in the mountains, where farming is impossible. But the snow melts in spring and summer, and water runs into the rivers. Those that flow eastward are used to irrigate the rich farming land of the High Plains.

History France claimed what is now eastern Colorado in 1682. Spanish explorers visited this land and finally claimed the whole region for their king in 1706. The explorers found many Indians already living in the region. The Arapaho, Cheyenne, Commanche, Kiowa, and Pawnee tribes lived on the plains. The Utes lived in the mountain valleys in the west.

France gained control of the whole region by a secret treaty with Spain. In 1803 the United States received the eastern half as part of the Louisiana Purchase. The western half became U.S. territory at the end of the Mexican War in 1848.

Gold was discovered ten years later in Cherry Creek (now in downtown Denver). Men from the East flocked to Colorado. Denver, Boulder, and Colorado City were among the first settlements.

The white men took land that the Indians had used for hunting. The Cheyenne and Arapaho of the plains fought to hold their hunting grounds. A group of soldiers attacked a Cheyenne village in 1864, in the battle now called the Sand Creek Massacre. Hundreds of Indian men, women, and children were killed.

The U.S. government criticized the soldiers' bloody attack. In the mountains, the Utes fought for their land, too. After many bitter fights, in which Indians and whites alike were killed, peace was finally made. Nearly all the Indians moved to reservations in other areas.

Colorado became the 38th state in 1876. Some of its people mined gold

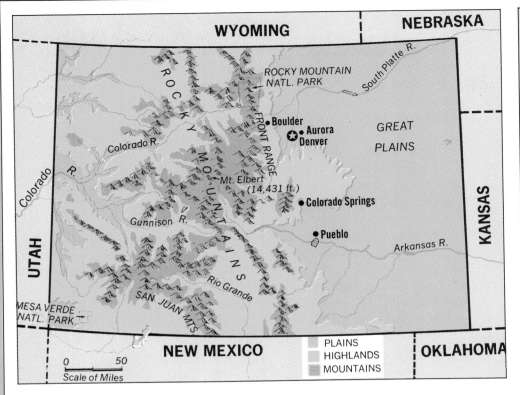

WYOMING NEBRASKA

ROCKY MOUNTAIN
NATL. PARK

South Platte R.

ROCKY

Colorado R.

FRONT RANGE

• Boulder
☆ • Aurora
Denver

GREAT
PLAINS

Colorado
R.

Mt. Elbert
(14,431 ft.)

• Colorado Springs

MOUNTAINS

Gunnison R.

• Pueblo

UTAH

KANSAS

Arkansas R.

Rio Grande

SAN JUAN MTS.

MESA VERDE
NATL. PARK

0   50

Scale of Miles

NEW MEXICO

PLAINS
HIGHLANDS
MOUNTAINS

OKLAHOMA

COLORADO

Capital and largest city
Denver (505,000 people)

Area
104,247 square miles (269,979 sq. km)
Rank: 8th

Population
3,301,000 people
Rank: 26th

Statehood
August 1, 1876
(38th state admitted)

Principal rivers
Colorado River
Arkansas River
South Platte River

Highest point
Mount Elbert; 14,433 feet (4,399 m)

Motto
Nil Sine Numine
("Nothing without Providence")

Song
"Where the Columbines Grow"

Famous people
Frederick Bonfils,
M. Scott Carpenter,
Douglas Fairbanks,
Florence Rena Sabin,
Lowell Thomas,
Paul Whiteman.

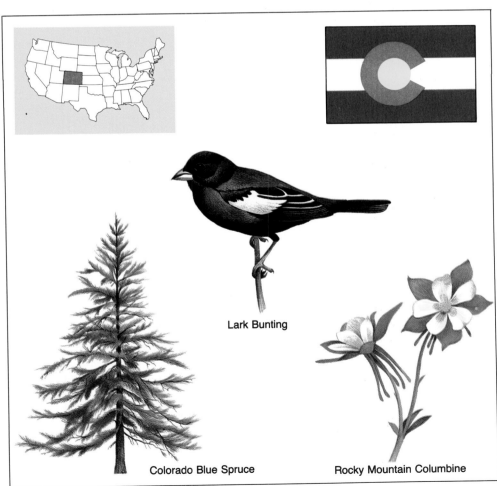

Lark Bunting

Colorado Blue Spruce

Rocky Mountain Columbine

The English chemist John Dalton was the first to study color blindness scientifically. He was color blind himself, which he had discovered as a small boy. He was watching a parade one day and the people around him were talking about the soldiers' red uniforms. He had thought they were green!

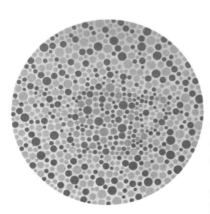

▲ *A red/green color blindness test card. If you have normal color vision you should be able to see a teapot.*

and silver in the mountains, and some raised sheep and cattle on the plains. But time brought changes. Other natural resources were discovered and mined. Irrigation brought farmers to the plains. People earned money and started factories.

Coloradans at Work   Manufacturing is the top industry of Colorado now. Among the principal manufactured goods are machinery, food products, computer equipment, aerospace equipment, rubber, and steel. Denver, the capital, and Pueblo are the main industrial cities in the state.

Pueblo has a huge steel industry. The city began in 1842 as a trading post of James P. Beckwourth, a black merchant. He named it *Pueblo* (Spanish for "town") because many of the people there were Mexicans.

Colorado has about 27,000 farms that range in size from large ranches to small vegetable farms. Cattle, sheep, and poultry are raised on the High Plains. The leading crops are wheat, corn, hay, and sugar beets.

Mining is a major industry in the state, which holds half the world's supply of molybdenum (a metal that hardens steel). Other important minerals are petroleum, natural gas, coal, and uranium. Oil shale is Colorado's main undeveloped resource.

Tourism ranks among the state's top industries. Millions of visitors come each year, attracted by Colorado's magnificent scenery, climate, and recreational facilities.

Rocky Mountain National Park covers 405 square miles (1,049 sq. km). The Great Divide runs through it. A fine road takes motorists more than two miles (3 km) above sea level. They can see ice fields glittering in summer sun. And they may catch sight of mountain lion, elk, black bear, and bighorn sheep. Mesa Verde (Green Table), another famous national park, has houses built high into cliffs by Indians of long ago. These houses were already very old when

the first white men arrived.

Skiers visit such well-known resorts as Aspen, Vail, and Winter Park. Fishermen, big-game hunters, and mountain climbers are attracted to these and other places in summer.

ALSO READ: CLIFF DWELLERS; GOLD RUSH; INDIANS, AMERICAN; INDIAN WARS; LOUISIANA PURCHASE; MEXICAN WAR; PIKE, ZEBULON; RIO GRANDE; WESTWARD MOVEMENT.

COLOR BLINDNESS   Some people do not distinguish colors so clearly as other people. These individuals are color blind. You must first understand how you see colors to understand what is meant by color blindness.

White light, or sunlight, is really a combination of different colors—red, orange, yellow, green, blue, indigo, and violet. Each of these colors can be produced by mixing three primary (basic) colors—red, green, and blue—in the right amounts. At the back of the eye is a type of screen called the retina. Some cells of the retina are sensitive to red, some to green, and some to blue light. When white light falls on the retina, it stimulates all three cell types more or less equally. The result is that you see white light. You see other colors when the retina cells are stimulated in unequal amounts. For example, you see a yellow color when the red and green cells are equally stimulated and the blue cells stimulated only very slightly.

Color blindness occurs when the sensitivity of the retina to any one of these colors is damaged. For example, when the cells sensitive to red are affected, a person cannot see red in quite the same way as a person whose sensitivity to red is normal. People who have the commonest types of color blindness generally see red and green as different degrees of yellow, but they see other colors normally.

Some people cannot see any color at all. Their world appears black, white, and gray. This condition is very rare. Color blindness affects men more than women. A color-blind person may be unaware of his condition unless his color vision is tested.

ALSO READ: COLOR, EYE, LIGHT, SIGHT.

COLUMBIA RIVER The Columbia River begins high in the ice and snow of the Canadian Rocky Mountains in British Columbia. It streams through mountain passes as it flows southward across the U.S. border into Washington state. Then it curves westward to empty into the Pacific Ocean at Astoria, Oregon. The Columbia River forms most of the boundary between Washington and Oregon. (See the map with the article on NORTH AMERICA.)

Robert Gray, an American sea captain, discovered the mouth of the river in 1792, while he was cruising along the Oregon coast in his ship, the *Columbia*. He named the river after the ship. The American explorers Meriwether Lewis and William Clark paddled their canoes through the rapids of the Columbia River to reach the Pacific in 1805. Within six years, another explorer, David Thompson, had traveled the entire 1,214 miles (1,954 km) of the Columbia, from source to mouth.

More than 25 dams have been built on the Columbia and its many tributaries. Among the largest are the Grand Coulee, Bonneville, John Day, McNary, and the Dalles. These dams harness the river's flow to make electricity. They also make the water flow into irrigation canals and form lakes where people can sail boats and swim.

Because of the dams, oceangoing ships can travel up the river only as far as Portland, Oregon. Small boats go around the dams by using canals, part of a 328-mile (528-km) slack-water navigation channel up the river. The Columbia River salmon get around the dams by jumping up "fish ladders." A fish ladder provides a water stairway for fish that go upstream to lay their eggs.

ALSO READ: BRITISH COLUMBIA, DAM, OREGON, RIVER, WASHINGTON.

COLUMBUS, CHRISTOPHER (1451–1506) Christopher Columbus was one of the courageous seafarers who followed their dreams right off the maps to unknown places. He opened the New World—North and South America—to all of Europe.

Columbus was born in Genoa, Italy, the son of a weaver. His name in Italian was Cristoforo Colombo. He was also called Cristóbal Colón when he sailed under the flag of Spain. Columbus made many voyages to the Gold Coast of Africa in his youth. The study of maps and his own sailing experience led him to believe that Asia could be reached by heading west. Europeans wanted an easier way to get Asia's gold, silk, and spices than by slow caravans crossing great mountains and deserts. Mapmakers and seamen thought that the voyage would be impossible.

▲ *Christopher Columbus, whose voyages to the Americas paved the way for the opening up of the New World.*

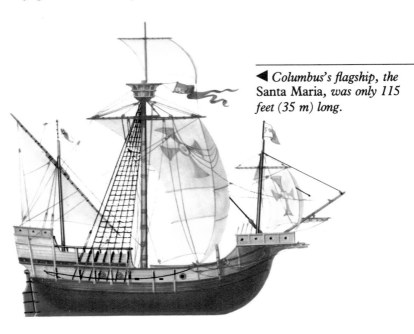

◄ *Columbus's flagship, the* Santa Maria, *was only 115 feet (35 m) long.*

▲ *Quanah Parker, famous Comanche chief. His first name means "sweet smelling one." He got his last name from his white mother.*

On Christmas Eve, 1492, a cabin boy was at the helm of the *Santa Maria* when the ship was wrecked. Columbus had to sail home to Spain in the *Niña*, beating the *Pinta*, the other ship of his fleet, by only a few hours.

Columbus tried to persuade King John I of Portugal to give him money for ships, but John refused. So Columbus went to Spain. After six years, Queen Isabella agreed to provide money for the expedition, and three ships sailed from Spain on August 3, 1492. They were the *Niña*, the *Pinta*, and the *Santa Maria*, which Columbus commanded. The voyage was difficult. The men grew discouraged and almost mutinied as they sailed farther and farther from home. Land was finally sighted on October 12. Columbus named the land San Salvador, claiming it for Spain. San Salvador was actually an island in the Bahamas, but Columbus always believed he had found the "Indies," and he called the people there "Indians." Upon his return to Spain, he was greeted with joy and given many honors.

Columbus made three more voyages, in 1493, 1498, and 1502. He established settlements and discovered new islands each time. Troubles in the colonies led to Columbus's arrest in 1500. He was soon pardoned, but his enemies were able to reduce the amount of money he was given for his fourth and last voyage. Columbus returned to Spain tired and ill from this voyage in 1504. He spent the last months of his life trying to collect the rewards due him, but he died in poverty. Years later Columbus's grandson had his remains moved from Spain to Santo Domingo, where they now lie in the cathedral of Santa Maria.

■ LEARN BY DOING

Columbus died unhappy, but he had started exploration that changed the world. His name lives on in rivers, nations, and cities. How many places can you find that were named after the man who opened the Americas to Europe? ■

ALSO READ: AMERICA, EXPLORATION, VIKINGS.

COMANCHE INDIANS The Comanche Indians were nomads of the Great Plains. They hunted bison (buffalo) as they wandered through the present-day states of Nebraska, Kansas, Oklahoma, Colorado, and Texas.

The Comanches were the best horsemen of all the Indians. They rode bareback (without a saddle). Each warrior braided a loop of horsehair into his horse's mane. If he was shot at, the warrior could slip his body into the loop and ride against his horse's side, with only one leg hooked over the top of his horse. Soldiers and pioneers claimed that a Comanche warrior could shoot as well from this horizontal position as sitting up on his horse.

Horses were so important to this tribe that they became a kind of money. A wealthy man would own several hundred horses. With a good horse, he could buy weapons, food, or even a wife! The Comanches roamed far and wide, always on the lookout for more horses. They caught and tamed wild horses and attacked Indian and white settlements alike to add to their wealth. Their buffalo-hide tepees were easily moved, so they could quickly pack up to follow the buffalo herd or look for new territory to raid.

As the white man moved west, he killed thousands and thousands of bison. The Comanches fought to save their land and way of life. But soon they could not find enough food by hunting. They signed a peace treaty with the United States government in 1867 and moved to a reservation in what is now the state of Oklahoma. They were given farming equipment. Today, many of the approximately 7,500 Comanches that live in the United States work as businessmen, ranchers, and farmers.

ALSO READ: BISON; INDIANS, AMERICAN; INDIAN WARS.

COMB JELLY Comb jellies are among the oddest animals in the ocean. They look like transparent jellyfish and are usually round or oval. One kind of comb jelly is the *sea walnut*. Another is the *sea gooseberry*, or "cat's eye," which is often washed onto beaches. You might find some about the size of a marble. Try placing a few cat's eyes in a pail of sea water. If they are not dead, they will swim around, gobbling up living things in the water.

Varieties of comb jellies live in oceans over most of the world, but most kinds inhabit warm waters. They are greedy eaters. They snare prey, such as fish and fish eggs, with sticky, hairy tentacles.

If you see them swim, you will notice tiny hairlike structures, called *cilia*, beat the water rapidly, moving the animals forward like tiny paddleboats. Eight sets of the cilia are arranged like teeth on a comb. The beating of the cilia refracts light in the water, causing rainbow colors to ripple as the animal swims. Comb jellies shine at night, making the water around them beautifully green and luminous.

Comb jellies form a group, or *phylum*, called the *Ctenophora*. Some of the 80 varieties are quite beautiful. One kind, *Venus's girdle*, is shaped like a ribbon and may grow to be 4 feet (1.2 m) in length.

ALSO READ: ANIMAL KINGDOM.

COMBUSTION see FIRE.

COMETS Comets are the strange nomads of the solar system that travel around the sun in very elongated paths. A comet first appears as a faint, moving spot far out in space. As it nears the sun, it becomes brighter and may grow a tail. After its closest approach to the sun, it begins to dim, and any tail formed soon disappears.

Some comets are seen every few years because their orbits are small, perhaps taking them only as far out as the planet Jupiter. These are too faint to be seen easily with the naked eye. The very bright comets move in much larger orbits and may take thousands of years to go around once. These often grow fine tails, but they move so quickly when near the sun that they may only be seen with the naked eye for a very few weeks.

The small solid nucleus of a comet is made mostly of water ice and frozen ammonia, methane, and carbon dioxide, all mixed with dust particles. The *Giotto* space probe photographed the nucleus of Halley's Comet as a "peanut" about nine miles (15 km) long. The tail forms when the ice is turned to vapor by the sun's heat, and dust particles are also released. A comet's tail may be millions of miles long and always points away from the sun.

People have been watching comets for many centuries. In 1705 the English astronomer Edmund Halley

The European *Giotto* and two Soviet *Vega* space probes showed details of the "dirty snowball" nucleus of Halley's Comet. They found that the dust coming off the nucleus contains complex carbon compounds. The nucleus of the comet was found to be about 9 miles (15 km) long, 5 miles (7.5 km) wide, and 5 miles (7.5 km) thick. Its surface is very black.

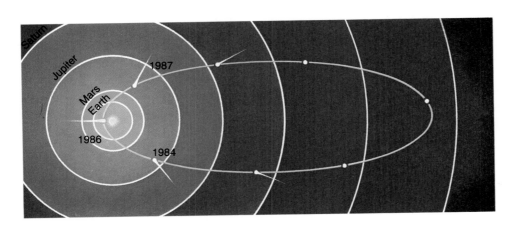

◄ *Halley's Comet is visible from Earth only once in every 76 years, most recently in 1986. This picture shows the path of the comet's orbit through the solar system. At its farthest from the sun it travels beyond the orbit of the planet Neptune.*

▲ *Always keep a lookout for comets—enormous streamers of glowing gas and dust. This picture shows Comet West, which broke into pieces in 1975.*

noted that the description of three comets—which had been seen in 1531, 1607, and 1682—were very much alike. Halley thought that it might really be just one comet, appearing again and again. If it were, he figured, it would appear again in about 75 or 76 years, or in 1758. It did, and the comet was named after him. Halley's Comet was spectacular in 1835 and 1910, but in 1986 it seemed faint, because the Earth was in the wrong part of its orbit for the best view.

ALSO READ: ORBIT, SOLAR SYSTEM, SPACE.

COMICS Every morning and evening millions of children and adults all over the world spend a few minutes reading their favorite comics, or "funnies," in their daily newspapers.

Most comics consist of a set of black and white or color drawings that tell a funny, exciting, or dramatic story. In a comic, what the character says or thinks is drawn in a "balloon" above him or her.

Artists draw comics for people of all ages and interests. Some comics are truly "funnies" that present characters who do and say funny things. One example is the comic strip *Blondie*, by Chic Young, which shows the amusing adventures of Blondie and her bumbling husband, Dagwood Bumstead. *Garfield* by Jim Davis presents the antics of a funny cat. Another kind is the adventure comic strip, which leaves its readers "hanging" in suspense so that they

will be sure to buy the next day's paper to find out what happens. *Steve Canyon*, by Milton A. Caniff, is an adventure strip about the exciting life of an Air Force colonel. One of several strips about fantastic, impossible adventures of bigger-than-life heroes is *Superman*, by Jerry Siegel.

Comic strips have been read and enjoyed for more than 75 years. The first comic strip, *Hogan's Alley*, by Richard F. Outcault, in which the main character was "the Yellow Kid," was published in 1896. *Hogan's Alley* was not actually a true comic strip, but really a full-page drawing.

Comic strips are printed in newspapers all over the world, but the "funnies" are most popular in the United States. A famous artist once said that the most original American art form is comics. Comics appear in almost every American newspaper. Artists sell their comics to a *syndicate*, a company that sells the comics to all newspapers that want to print them. Other comics are printed in books called comic books.

ALSO READ: CARTOONING, COMMERCIAL ART, DESIGN, DRAWING, GRAPHIC ARTS, NEWSPAPER.

COMMERCIAL ART Have you ever made a sign for a lemonade stand saying "LEMONADE—TEN CENTS A GLASS"? Or painted a poster advertising a school fair? If you have, you have made some commercial art. The word "commercial" comes from commerce, which means business. Commercial art, then, is that art which has to do with business.

▼ *The amusing adventures of Charlie Brown are told in* Peanuts, *one of the most popular of all comic strips. It was created in 1950 by a cartoonist from Minnesota, Charles Schulz.*

The Romans had commercial art over two thousand years ago. They put signs over shops so that people could tell what was sold inside. A huge shoe would hang outside a shoe-maker's shop, for example. Many shops have similar signs in Europe today. A carved wooden Indian indicated a cigar store years ago in the United States.

Commercial artists must be able to design, draw, and paint well. They often receive training at an art school or college. They learn how to lay out magazines and books—that is, where to put the pictures and columns of type, how to arrange everything on a page. They learn how to design jackets for books and how to illustrate them. Some commercial artists learn mechanical drawing or drafting (drawing of architectural or engineering diagrams), map and chart drawing, graphic arts (print making, engraving, etching), and cartooning.

Commercial artists, working with a special writer called a *copywriter*, prepare advertisements for magazines and newspapers and commercials for television. They design and illustrate books. Fashion designers design clothing, and industrial designers—working with engineers—design the shapes of appliances and many other products.

ALSO READ: ADVERTISING, CARTOONING, DESIGN, FASHION, GRAPHIC ARTS, MECHANICAL DRAWING.

COMMON COLD We have all suffered the headache, sore throat, sneezing, stuffy nose, cough, and fever of a cold. The common cold is one of our most widespread diseases.

Many people think that colds are caused by getting chilled or damp. It is true that a person who is weakened by a chill may catch a cold more easily. But scientists have found that colds are caused by tiny organisms called *viruses*. Hand contact with a person having a cold is the worst

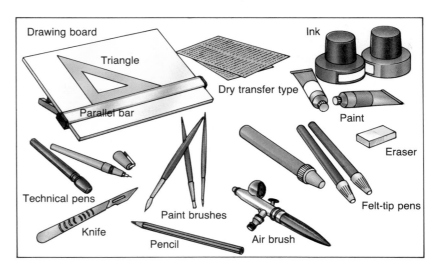
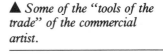

spreader of these viruses. They are carried through the air by coughs or sneezes too. Anybody nearby may catch the cold if the viruses enter the nose or mouth. That is why it is important to cover the nose and mouth when coughing or sneezing.

More than 100 different cold viruses have been discovered, and many more may exist. It is very difficult to make a vaccine that stops so many different germs. Scientists are looking for other ways to protect people against cold viruses. One idea is to use chemicals that attack the viruses. Another idea is to use drugs that strengthen the body's natural defenses against the viruses.

▲ *Some of the "tools of the trade" of the commercial artist.*

Norman Rockwell was probably the best-known American illustrator. He gained great popularity as a cover illustrator for *The Saturday Evening Post* and other magazines. Rockwell also worked for many advertisers during his long life—he died in 1978 at the age of 84.

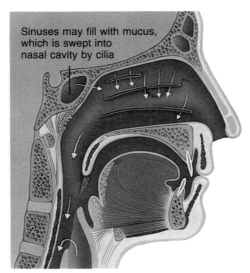

▲ *The common cold is a virus that affects the linings of the nose, sinuses, and sometimes the throat and bronchi.*

But no effective cure for a common cold has yet been found. Most people follow a simple method of treatment that prevents the cold from developing into a more serious lung illness, such as bronchitis or pneumonia. This involves rest and drinking plenty of liquids. If the patient has a high fever, he or she usually rests in bed and takes aspirin to relieve pain and reduce the fever.

Many people miss several days of school or work a year because they have to stay home to treat a cold.

ALSO READ: ANTIGEN AND ANTIBODY, DISEASE, VIRUS.

COMMON MARKET see EUROPEAN COMMUNITY.

COMMONWEALTH OF NATIONS If you live in Canada, you are a member of an independent country that governs itself much like the United States. But it is also part of the Commonwealth of Nations. This is a group of countries that were once all part of the British Empire. Britain does not govern them any more, but they continue to use systems of law based on those of Britain, and have a common interest in each other. Member nations of the Commonwealth talk over problems and have agreements for trade and defense.

For more than one hundred years, Britain ruled so many colonies all around the globe that a common saying was, "The sun never sets on the British Empire." (Can you figure out why not?) When colonies in the empire began to want freedom—beginning with Canada in the 1860's—Britain saw that it either had to loosen its ties or lose these colonies.

Canada, Australia, New Zealand, and South Africa were free nations by 1931. But they decided to form a special relationship with their mother country, Britain. These four countries became the first independent members of the Commonwealth of Nations. After World War II, Britain granted independence to many of its colonies in Asia, Africa, and the Americas. Nearly all of these new nations joined the Commonwealth. (The Republic of Ireland, South Africa, and Pakistan withdrew from it.) In 1986, the Commonwealth had 49 independent members and more than 20 other members, known as dependent territories or associated states.

Britain's Queen Elizabeth II is head of state of the United Kingdom (Britain) and 17 other countries. She is also head of the Commonwealth, but she does not have any real power. She is a symbol, or representative, of the Commonwealth. Each of the member countries in the Commonwealth chooses its own government and makes its own decisions on things like peace and war.

ALSO READ: COLONY, ENGLISH HISTORY.

COMMUNICATION Communication is an exchange of information, feelings, attitudes, or ideas. Many animals communicate with one another, but humans have the most complicated system of communication. Speech, writing, books, magazines, mail, telephone, radio, and television all work together to set human beings apart from every other living thing. Without communication there would be no recorded history, no development of civilization, no organization of society, and no learning. Each new generation would have to discover and invent everything again.

Every time you talk to your family or to a friend, you are communicating by *speech*, the earliest and still the most important kind of human communication. We will never know how or when speech began—we can only guess. The earliest people probably communicated much like other animals—by grunts. Hundreds of thousands of years ago, people somehow learned to use sounds, each of which meant something special to other people. They slowly learned to put the sounds together to form language.

People still had two big problems. They could not communicate over distances, and as soon as a person spoke, the words vanished. People began to use runners to solve the first problem. But if the message had to go 30 miles (48 km), even the fastest runner needed over 3 hours to carry it. So people kept trying to find faster ways to carry messages.

Written Communication To solve the second problem, people first invented ways of making pictures, from which picture writing developed. The first people to do this were the Sumerians, in about 3500 B.C. Soon after that, the ancient Egyptians developed another important picture writing, called *hieroglyphics*, which was used in religious and royal writing. Simplified hieroglyphics were used in government and business. The first alphabet was developed by the Syrians in about 1300 B.C. Alphabet writing lets us express many more ideas than does picture writing.

People were soon busy writing, first on clay tablets, then on rolled-up sheets or scrolls of papyrus made from reeds (plant fiber) and later on parchment made from animal skin. People began to change from scrolls to books around A.D. 200. Books were easier to read and store. But each book had to be lettered by hand, and they were expensive.

Printing is one of the greatest inventions. The oldest known printed work is a scroll printed with carved wooden blocks in Korea in about A.D. 700. Europeans did not use printing until the fifteenth century. Johannes Gutenberg, a German, invented a usable system of movable type around 1440. With Gutenberg's system, each letter was a separate piece. A book page could be made up of type *set* in a frame, and many copies could be made. Books could be produced more quickly and cheaply, so that many more people could read and learn from the communication of others.

Printing also brought about new forms of communication, especially newspapers and magazines. Newspapers as we know them today began in the seventeenth century, magazines in the eighteenth century.

Modern Devices New discoveries to help communication occurred in the nineteenth century, too. The invention of cameras and film allowed people to make an exact visual record of what they saw. Later in the century, inventors devised ways to show movement on film by making motion pictures.

Electricity in communication added a new dimension that is becoming as important as printing. Electricity made communication over huge distances possible. The telegraph was the first communication device to use electricity. It sent signals over wires. Samuel F. B. Morse sent the first message by telegraph in 1844. Wires were later used to send the human voice over a long distance. Alexander Graham Bell patented this new device, the telephone, in 1876. Then people learned to use electricity to transmit voices without wires. Guglielmo Marconi first demonstrated the "wireless," or radio, in 1895.

In the 1900's, people have invented other devices to help them communicate. Most astounding are television,

▲ *An Egyptian papyrus of the 1200's* B.C. *Hieroglyphic, the written language of the ancient Egyptians, was made up of picture symbols.*

▲ *An early newspaper,* The Antwerp Gazette, *published on June 17, 1621.*

◄ *Johannes Gutenberg, the inventor of printing from movable type, checks a printed sheet. This relief is from the Gutenberg monument in Mainz, Germany.*

▲ *A telephone of 1905. Telephones quickly replaced the telegraph as a means of rapid communication.*

▲ *A crystal radio set of the 1920's.*

▼ *Many organizations now use video for training new recruits. By recording lectures and demonstrations on tape, they can be replayed many times over to different groups.*

which uses electricity to transmit sound and pictures, and communications satellites, which from far out in space can send television and other kinds of communications anywhere in the world.

People have also learned how to make a permanent record of sound, just as they learned to make written and visual records. Thomas Edison invented the phonograph in 1877. Later, sound recordings were combined with moving pictures.

Computers that process information with blinding speed have given communication another huge push forward. With a computer, people can store, process, and print information faster than ever before and in enormous quantities. A computer can print a million words in as little as a minute and store the words on a single disc only a few inches across.

Uses of Communication People have become fascinated by communication, and scientists have begun to study it. One important fact that scientists have discovered is that many animals communicate, too. Bees and other insects "tell" one another where flowers are blooming by performing movements like a dance when they return to the hive. Birds sing and call to one another with various meanings. And dolphins, members of the whale family, seem to have a very complicated language that some scientists hope they can translate.

Scientists divide human communication into *personal* and *mass* communication. A message is carried from *sender* to *receiver* by a *channel* or *medium*. Personal communication takes place whenever one person exchanges ideas with another. In mass communication, one person (or a group of people) sends a message to many people whom the sender never sees. Its channels, called *mass media*, include newspapers, books, radio, television, films, and recordings.

Every successful communication

has five parts. These five parts can best be expressed in the following question. *Who* says *what* to *whom* through what *channel* or *medium*, and what is the *result*? If you do not understand what someone says, communication fails. If you hear and understand someone but decide to ignore what is being said, is the communication a success or failure?

People have more ways and better ways to communicate now than ever before. But many problems—both personal and worldwide—are caused because people still do not always understand one another. Scientists continue to learn more about the process of communication.

For further information on:
Animal Communication, *see* ANIMAL VOICES, DOLPHINS AND PORPOISES.
History, *see* ANCIENT CIVILIZATIONS; BELL, ALEXANDER GRAHAM; GUTENBERG, JOHANNES; MARCONI, GUGLIELMO; MORSE, SAMUEL F. B.; RADIO BROADCASTING; SUMER; TELEVISION BROADCASTING.
Language, *see* ALPHABET, HIEROGLYPHICS, LANGUAGES, WRITTEN LANGUAGE.
Modern Devices, *see* COMPUTER, RADIO, TAPE RECORDER, FACSIMILE, PHOTOCOPIER, TELECOMMUNICATIONS, TELEGRAPH, TELEPHONE, TELEVISION.
Printing, *see* BOOK, MAGAZINE, NEWSPAPER, PRINTING, PUBLISHING, TYPESETTING.

COMMUNICATIONS SATELLITE Television covers sports and news around the world. Until 1964, reporters in distant countries had to race to the nearest airport with their news film. An airplane carried the film to the United States. The plane trip took from half a day to several days, and the film showed news that was old by the time it appeared on television. Telephone calls across the ocean were hard to make because the calls went by cables that lay on the ocean floor. But there weren't always enough cables, so people often waited hours to call somebody in another country. Satellites used for communications have changed that. The first one was put into orbit around the Earth in 1964.

Today, television stations show videotapes of news events in other countries on the same day the event happens. Events can even be broadcast "live," no matter where in the world they happen. And telephone calls to almost any country in the world take just a minute or two.

Communications satellites orbit, or circle, the Earth about 22,300 miles (35,900 km) above the equator. At that height, a satellite stays above one place on the Earth's surface, even though the satellite is moving faster than the Earth is turning.

A communications satellite is a relay station, or switchboard, in space. Television reaches the United States from Europe through the switchboard. First, the signal goes by cable to a ground station in Europe. The station antenna transmits (sends) the signal in a straight line to a satellite above the Atlantic Ocean. The satellite automatically sends the signal back down to the antenna at a station in the United States. Finally, the signal goes by cable to the television

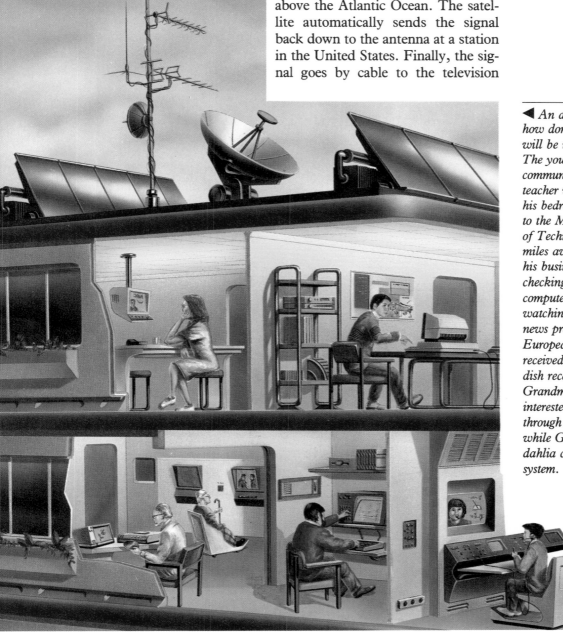

◄ *An artist's impression of how domestic communications will be in the next century. The youngest child is in direct communication with his school teacher while his brother, in his bedroom upstairs, is linked to the Massachusetts Institute of Technology hundreds of miles away. Their father runs his business from home. He is checking stock through his computer. Their mother is watching her favorite daytime news program. It is a European program and is received through the satellite dish receiver on the roof. The Grandmother keeps an interested eye on the street through closed circuit television while Grandfather refers to a dahlia catalog on his video system.*

▲ *Giant antennas such as this one receive the signals or programs relayed by Intelsat, a modern news satellite system. Several satellites work together in the system, so that their signal beams combine to cover the whole world surface.*

network. The whole trip takes one-fourth of a second.

Japan is much farther from the U.S. than Europe, so two satellites are needed to get a signal from the U.S. to Japan. An Atlantic satellite sends the signal to a Pacific satellite. Then the Pacific satellite sends the signal down to a station in Japan.

Satellites relay telephone calls the same way. One satellite can carry many more calls than one telephone cable. It is now easier and cheaper to talk to people around the world.

Today there are many communications satellites around Earth. Many homes have their own dish antennas to receive TV programs from satellites.

ALSO READ: ORBIT, SATELLITE, SPACE RESEARCH, TELEPHONE.

COMMUNISM The idea of Communism is very ancient. But Communism, as it is known today, first became popular in Europe in the 1800's. Put very simply, Communism is a system of government in which everything is owned by all the people. The people are represented by the state, or central government.

Communism grew out of the misery and poverty that existed in Europe after the Industrial Revolution. During this time, factories replaced many small businesses. The machines created new jobs, and thousands of people traveled to crowded cities to find work. Factory bosses often treated their workers harshly. Employees had to work long hours in dangerous conditions for small wages.

Two German scholars, Karl Marx and Friedrich Engels, wrote a book called the *Communist Manifesto* in 1848. Marx and Engels believed all people should work for the common good. They made popular the Communist motto, "from each according to his ability, to each according to his need." They wrote of a "classless society," in which no single group of people would be more powerful than any other.

The Communists, unlike the Socialists who shared similar ideas, believed in revolution and violence to accomplish their goals. The first major Communist revolution took place in Russia (now the Soviet Union) in 1917. It was led by Vladimir (sometimes called Nikolai) Lenin. Another important Communist nation today is the People's Republic of China.

Communism as Marx thought of it does not exist anywhere today. Marx believed that, in the end, people would be able to live together without a central government. But in many Communist countries the government has become extremely powerful. It owns most of the property and industry in the nation in the name of the people. What is good for the country is believed to be more important than the freedom of the individual person. People are not allowed to believe or behave as they wish. However, during the last years of the 1980's, the U.S.S.R. under Mikhail Gorbachev adopted a freer form of communism. Then, in 1989, the peoples of most eastern European countries overthrew their strict communist rulers and demanded more democratic government.

ALSO READ: CAPITALISM; CHINA; ECONOMICS; INDUSTRIAL REVOLUTION; LENIN, NIKOLAI; MARX, KARL; SOCIALISM; SOVIET UNION.

▼ *Huge military parades are held in Red Square, Moscow, on May Day (May 1). May Day is celebrated in many Communist countries to honor the workers.*

COMMUNITY Animals or people that live together as a group form a community. In the animal world, communities include packs of wolves, herds of elephants, and prides of lions. Social insects, such as bees in their hives and ants in their colonies, also form communities.

Most people belong to several communities. The *family* community usually has mother, father, and children. The *neighborhood* community is the area where the family lives. People also belong to the *state* community, the *national* community, and the *world*, or international community. Each of these communities is part of the next larger community.

The people of a community have similar ways and customs. For example, people in a neighborhood live in similar houses and apartments, and most people in state and national communities speak the same language. A community is usually in a definite space—a house at a certain address, a state with a name and boundaries, a nation at a certain spot on the globe, a world at a certain spot in the universe.

Each community is run by rules or laws. A family decides when children have to go to bed, or what time to have dinner. A state has laws such as who must go to school and for how many years. And each community has certain activities or problems that unite it. For example, all the people in a neighborhood on the shore of an ocean may earn their living by fishing. People in a jungle village might get together to protect themselves from wild animals.

The earliest communities of people started thousands of years ago. Ancient peoples were hunters who were always searching for food. People hunted animals, fished, and gathered wild plants and fruit. If they could not collect enough food, they starved. Then, perhaps 15,000 years ago, people discovered they could raise crops.

Somebody, probably in the region that is now Syria and Iraq, noticed that plants grew where seeds had fallen. People began settling down in one spot, in communities. Women planted seeds and farmed, while men hunted. The hunting and harvesting of crops started the first permanent community.

One of the earliest permanent communities was a town later called Jericho, located in what is now Israel. The people who settled there built mud houses and put up a wall around their town. They dug irrigation ditches to water their crops of wheat, barley, and flax.

Now that they had finally settled down in one spot, people found that they could raise animals and kill them for food. They also found that the community needed people who did not grow food, such as shopkeepers, artists, and priests. Farming communities gradually sprang up all along the Tigris and Euphrates rivers (now in Syria and Iraq), and along the Nile River in Egypt. The farmers noticed that each year the rivers flooded and left rich mountain soil on their farmlands. The farmers had no reason to move anymore, because the rivers brought new soil each year and crops were always good. Generation after generation of people stayed in the same place.

▲ *Community buying and selling flourishes unchanged in a market in Benares, India, where traders still sell grain as they have for centuries.*

▼ *Tokyo—a modern city—resembles many other modern cities and faces many of the same problems. Cities are large, dense communities; within them are a collection of smaller communities.*

More than half the total value of exports from the Comoros comes from vanilla, the flavoring that is used in ice cream, chocolate, pastry, and candy. The vanilla plant is a climbing orchid that makes its seeds in pods. The pods are picked before they are ripe. Then they are dried, chopped up, and soaked in alcohol and water to make vanilla essence. The word "vanilla" is Spanish for "little pod."

Finally, too many people were trying to live off the narrow strips of good land along the banks of the rivers. Some had to move back from the best farming areas. The people who moved farther away from the rivers did not know about fertilizers or crop rotation, so the soil quickly wore out. People tried to improve the soil by burning vegetation and using the ashes as fertilizer. But this process took a lot of time, and many farmers gave up. They left their villages and went elsewhere, burning forests and planting seeds between the burned stumps. They finally blazed their way through most of the forests of central Europe.

Some of the early farm communities, however, proved to be quite permanent. These farmers grew fruits, such as olives, dates, figs, and grapes. But the wheat farmers were constantly moving. These wheat farmers have been called *Danubians* because they followed the route of the Danube River. They made their way into Russia, Denmark, Sweden, and England. Others settled along the Swiss lakes and built houses on the water on piles of wood. Still other Danubians formed communities along the banks of the Rhine River.

People today have many more communities than they had thousands of years ago. Towns, cities, states, and nations are spread out in an ever-growing world community. But the first two communities—the family and the neighborhood—are still very much with us. And they are still the same, in many ways, as they were thousands of years ago.

For further information on:
Community Activities, *see* CLUBS AND SOCIETIES, FIRE FIGHTING, HOSPITAL, MUSEUM, POLICE, POSTAL SERVICE, PUBLIC HEALTH, PUBLIC UTILITY, SCHOOL, SOCIAL WORK.
General Community Life, *see* CITIZENSHIP, COMMUNICATION, CRIME, JUVENILE DELINQUENCY, LAW, SAFETY, SHELTER, TRAFFIC PLANNING, TRANSPORTATION.
History, *see* ANCIENT CIVILIZATIONS; CULTURE; CUSTOMS; FEUDALISM; INDIANS, AMERICAN; PIONEER LIFE.
Kinds of Communities, *see* CITY, COLONY, COUNTY, INTERNATIONAL RELATIONS, LOCAL GOVERNMENT, NATION, SUBURB.

COMORO ISLANDS The Comoro Islands are a volcanic *archipelago* (cluster of islands) in the Indian Ocean between north Madagascar and East Africa. Njazidja (which was called Grand Comoro until 1977) is the largest island. It has an active volcano, Mont Kartala, which erupted in 1977, making 20,000 people homeless.

The islands have a tropical climate. Most people are poor and earn their living from farming. Most of the farms are small and yields are gener-

COMORO ISLANDS

Capital City: Moroni (20,000 people).
Area: 838 square miles (2,171 sq. km).
Population: 500,000.
Government: Federal Islamic Republic.
Natural Resources: Lumber.
Export Products: Vanilla, copra, cloves, essential oils (for use in perfume).
Unit of Money: Comorian franc.
Official Languages: Arabic, French.

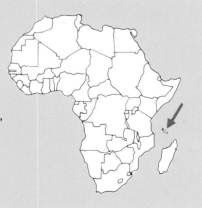

ally low, because the soils are infertile. The export crops, including vanilla, copra, and cloves, are grown on large plantations. The official languages are Arabic and French, but most people speak Comoran, a mixture of the East African language Swahili and Arabic.

Arabs ruled the islands until the French gained control of them in 1886. In 1975, France granted independence to the largely Muslim islands of Njazidja, Nzwani (formerly called Anjouan), and Mwali (formerly Mohéli). These islands now form the Federal Islamic Republic of the Comoros. The fourth major island, Mayotte, is largely Christian. Its people chose to remain under French control.

ALSO READ: AFRICA, INDIAN OCEAN.

COMPACT DISC A silvery disc only 5 inches (12 cm) across can play more than an hour of music. This is a compact disc, and it gives music of superb quality.

A compact disc contains a *digital* recording of music. This means that the sound is recorded in the form of code signals. The codes consist of millions of patterns of tiny pits on the surface of the disc. In a compact disc player, a laser beam of light moves

▼ *In a compact disc player, the laser beam picks up signals from the tiny surface pits on the disc (inset).*

across the disc as it spins and is reflected by the tiny surface pits. The reflected beam carries the signals, which are then changed into the music. Because there is no abrasive contact between the disc and the beam, there is no wear and tear on the disc. The quality is also improved because digital recordings are less prone to distortion, noise, and speed changes.

Compact discs have other uses. They can play many hours of speech instead of hours of music and may contain whole books read for blind people. Another type of compact disc with a television set can play back pictures as well as music. Compact discs can also be used to store information for computers. A disc can hold over 100,000 pages of data.

ALSO READ: RECORDING.

COMPASS Voyages of exploration and treks through unmapped wilderness would have been much more difficult without the simple device called the compass. A compass is a direction finder. Most compasses consist of a short, flat, thin, arrow-shaped piece of metal that is balanced on the point of a short rod. The rod sticks up from a circular card on which are printed the directions—north (N), south (S), east (E), and west (W). The piece of metal is a *magnet*. It can swing around on the rod, so the arrowhead points northward and the back of the arrow points southward. This happens because the Earth itself is a huge magnet, and one magnet always acts with force upon another.

Compasses are used in navigation. The Chinese were among the first to use the compass, and European sailors were using them by the 1100's. These sailors knew about a kind of iron ore called *lodestone*, which is a natural magnet. The first compasses they used were needle-shaped pieces of lodestone hanging by a thread.

Sailors also learned that they could make a magnet from an iron needle

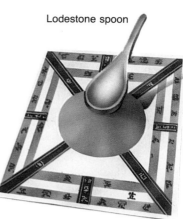

▲ *A lodestone spoon. In about 100 B.C. the Chinese discovered that if spoons made of the magnetic material lodestone were spun, they came to rest with the handles pointing in the same direction.*

▼ *The Earth acts like a giant magnet, with its poles near, but not at, the North and South Poles.*

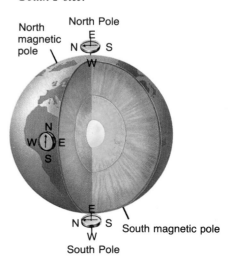

stroked on lodestone. They thrust the needle through a piece of reed or cork and floated it in water. One end of the needle turned toward the north.

■ **LEARN BY DOING**

You can use your watch as a compass. Point the hour hand at the sun. Bisect (cut in two) the angle between 12 o'clock and the hour hand and you have the direction of south. This works because the sun travels from east to west in about 12 hours. It travels 90° and is due south by 12 noon. During the same time the hour hand of the watch travels 180°—that is, through twice as big an angle. So, by halving the angle, you are slowing down the hand to match the speed of the sun. ■

The North Magnetic Pole Although the Earth's magnetism makes one end of a compass needle point

▲ *A decorated ivory compass.*

▶ *A modern army compass in a protective case.*

northward, the needle does not point straight to the North Pole, but to the *north magnetic pole*. This is a point located in the Canadian Northwest Territories, several hundred miles south of the actual North Pole. But the error of the compass can be corrected because navigators have measured the variations for almost all places on the Earth.

A *gyrocompass* is one that can be made to point always true north—or any other direction wanted. It consists of a *gyroscope* mounted so that it can swing freely. The gyroscope's wheel is started spinning and is pointed straight north. No matter in what direction a ship, airplane, or rocket turns, the gyrocompass mounted on it continues to point to the direction in which it was set.

ALSO READ: GYROSCOPE, MAGNET, NAVIGATION, NORTH POLE.

COMPOSER A man or woman who makes up music is a composer. If you make up a little melody to hum, you are composing a tune. If you play some notes on the piano just for fun, you are beginning to compose. But after you find sounds you like, the notes should be written down.

■ **LEARN BY DOING**

Have you ever wanted to compose a song? One way to begin is by taking a favorite poem and thinking up music to go with the words. If you know how to play a musical instrument, you probably know how to write down the song on music paper. If you have a tape recorder, you can sing or whistle the tune that you have made up in your head. Someone else could then help you write out your song by playing back the tape. ■

Composers use *tones*, or sounds, to write music. They combine them in different ways, using one at a time or many tones together. They use *rhythm,* so that some sounds move quickly while others are heard for a longer time. Composers can use human voices as well as many musical instruments, combining them to make interesting tones. They may combine all the instruments and voices into a large work for chorus and orchestra. Or they may want just the piano, or the violin, to play a piece of music. They are then writing a *solo* for that instrument.

Some composers can make up music without studying composition, but most people have to learn to use the sounds and rhythms that go into music. They study how different tones go together in the system of scales and keys (harmony). They learn to play the piano and perhaps other musical instruments. They learn what notes men or women can sing. When composers know these things, they are able to use them in their own way, to

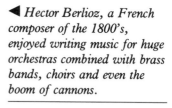

◄ *Hector Berlioz, a French composer of the 1800's, enjoyed writing music for huge orchestras combined with brass bands, choirs and even the boom of cannons.*

create music which sounds, when it is played, just as they "hear" it in their minds.

Composers use special paper ruled for musical notation, the written language of music. They write symbols for notes on the lines and spaces. Each note shows which sound is to be played and for how long. There are also symbols for "rests" of various lengths at points where the composer wants no sound at all. Composers show what key or *tonality* the piece needs. They then add signs telling whether the music is to be loud or soft, whether it is to slow down or speed up, and many other things.

◄ *The young Wolfgang Amadeus Mozart. Mozart wrote almost a thousand works—more than any other classical composer—before his death at the age of 35.*

▼ *Karlheinz Stockhausen is a modern composer whose music includes electronic and other sounds as well as traditional instruments.*

▲ *Although George Frederick Handel ranks as one of England's greatest composers, he was actually German and did not come to England until the age of 24.*

Stephen Foster was one of America's best-loved songwriters—he wrote favorites such as "Swanee River," "Oh! Susanna," and "My Old Kentucky Home." He never had any music lessons, but by the age of six he had taught himself to play the clarinet. Foster wrote more than 200 songs, many of which were hummed by people all over the world, but he died in poverty in New York City in 1860.

This collection of symbols is called a *music manuscript.*

The manuscripts of famous composers are very valuable. They are often kept in libraries and museums where music students may study them. Some composers today use a music typewriter, called a *music-writer,* instead of drawing musical notes by hand.

Some Famous Composers Music goes back to very ancient times, but little is known about actual pieces of music written before the 1200's and 1300's. Some of the earliest known composers wrote music for church services. *Musicologists,* students of music history, have been able to learn about many of the composers who have written music since that time.

Many countries have had great composers whose music became internationally known. Johann Sebastian Bach, Ludwig van Beethoven, Johannes Brahms, Felix Mendelssohn, Robert Schumann, and Richard Wagner were from Germany. Franz Joseph Haydn, Wolfgang Amadeus Mozart, Franz Schubert, and Johann Strauss were from Austria. Sergei Prokofiev, Sergei Rachmaninoff, Igor Stravinsky, and Peter I. Tchaikovsky were Russian. Frédéric Chopin was Polish. George Frederick Handel was a German who worked in England. Franz Liszt of Hungary, Edvard Grieg of Norway, Guiseppe Verdi of Italy, and Claude Debussy of France became internationally known composers. America has also produced many famous composers, including Stephen Foster, John Philip Sousa, George and Ira Gershwin, George M. Cohan, Irving Berlin, and Aaron Copland. You may read about these composers in this encyclopedia. Today, many younger composers are developing electronic music and are exploring new ways of writing music. Some composers have created new and different styles of music. Others are famous because they brought one style to its highest development.

Many composers write music in each century. Some become famous while they are alive but are forgotten later. Sometimes the music is appreciated only after the composer dies. The music of some composers is widely played and praised, and then forgotten. Long afterward it may be discovered again and become popular. For example, Bach's music was forgotten by most people for nearly a hundred years after his death. Interest in his work was revived in the 1800's.

ALSO READ: ART, ELECTRONIC MUSIC, MUSIC, OPERA. *For individual composers, see Index.*

COMPOSITION In writing, "composition" means "to put a story down on paper." Perhaps in the first and second grades, you and your classmates wrote a story together in reading class. The teacher really did the writing on a huge sheet of paper in front of the class. You all told her what words to use, and she printed them on the paper. It is surprising what a good story a class can write together.

You can write a composition by yourself. Instead of having the class give you ideas, you supply the ideas out of your head. This is easier than you think—if you write about a subject you like. You have to have a subject before you start to write. So, first of all, think about something you really like—swimming, camping, Little League baseball, friends on the playground, for instance. Remember, to interest the reader, the writer must be interested in the subject.

To tell your story, you must have a form that holds it together. There must be a beginning, a middle, and an end. If you think of a good way to start your story, you are well on your way. Sometimes the middle part is the hardest, filling out the body of the composition after your great start. Move on to finish your composition by writing the end. The end should tie together with the beginning of your story.

Your story should have some *sequence*—the sentences should follow one another in good order. You can help show sequence by using paragraphs. Start a new paragraph for the beginning, the middle, and the end. You may want even more paragraphs, depending on how much you have to say.

Pick a topic and write a composition. Need a subject? How about "My New Friend," "My Pet," "My Favorite Animal," "A Mysterious Happening." Remember that all writing is just talk written down. Sometimes it's more fun than talking, because you have more time to plan it out. And writing lasts when talk is forgotten.

ALSO READ: GRAMMAR, LANGUAGE ARTS, LETTER WRITING, PUNCTUATION, SPELLING, VOCABULARY.

COMPOUND see CHEMISTRY.

COMPUTER How long would it take you to add together $1+2+3+4+5$ and so on up to 1000? Even if you worked quickly, it would take you a long time to get the answer (500,500). Besides, you would have to do each of the thousand additions correctly or you would wind up with the wrong answer after all that hard work.

With a home computer, you would need about a minute to key in the program or instructions it needs. The computer would then do the additions in about one second. And it would always be right.

To "compute" means to count or to figure. A computer is a machine that solves problems many times faster than a person can. A computer does not think, so a person must give information to the computer, supply instructions on how to solve the problem, and tell in what form the answer is to be given.

Computers can answer many kinds of problems, and they can also store and handle information. They have played a most important role in the space program and in weather forecasting, where answers are needed quickly. If these answers had to be worked out by hand, they would not be ready for days or weeks. Some problems are so complicated that a person would need a hundred years to solve one of them!

Libraries, schools, hospitals, police, and businesses use computers to save many hours of searching through files. Imagine giving a librarian your topic for a science project and getting a list of useful books in a second! Doctors are using computers more and more. Computers keep records on hospital patients and provide up-to-date information on medicines and their effects on certain diseases. Computers can even help doctors to find out the cause of an illness. They can stop the countdown for a space launch if a part is not working right. The computer keeps the spacecraft in

▲ *It seems almost impossible that tiny chips such as this one can do the work of the enormous machine shown below.*

▼ *ENIAC, completed in 1946, was the first really electronic machine. It had 18,000 vacuum tubes that kept burning out at an alarming rate.*

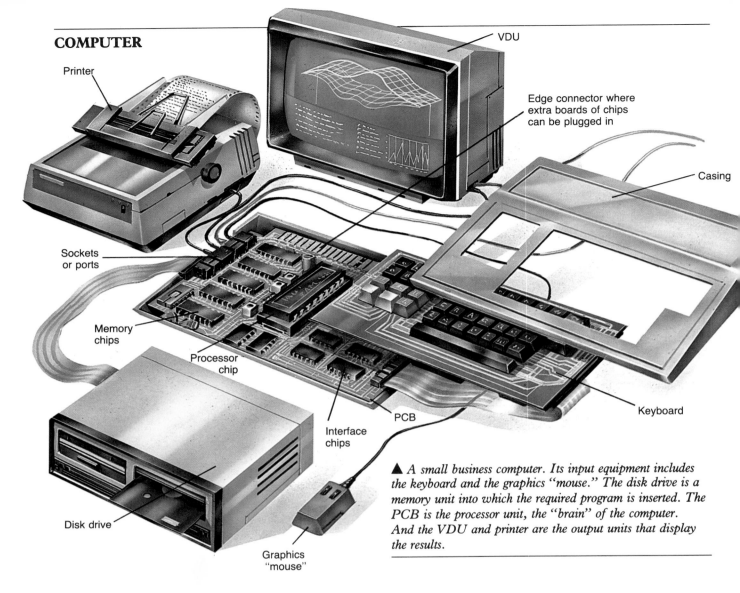

Printer

VDU

Edge connector where extra boards of chips can be plugged in

Casing

Sockets or ports

Memory chips

Processor chip

Interface chips

PCB

Keyboard

Disk drive

Graphics "mouse"

▲ *A small business computer. Its input equipment includes the keyboard and the graphics "mouse." The disk drive is a memory unit into which the required program is inserted. The PCB is the processor unit, the "brain" of the computer. And the VDU and printer are the output units that display the results.*

the correct flight path by constantly controlling its speed and direction. Computers can also write and perform music, check income tax, create pictures, and play games of all kinds, especially chess.

The First Computer Charles Babbage (1792–1871), an Englishman, was the first to think of a machine that could be given information and instructions to solve arithmetic problems. He worked on it for almost 38 years, but at that time no one could make the complex parts needed for his computer. Babbage never did build his machine, but the computers we use today are based on his ideas and designs.

It was not until electronics developed that a computer could be made.

The first electronic computer was a British computer called COLOSSUS, which was invented in 1943. It was built during World War II to crack enemy coded messages. However, it could not do any other task. The first general-purpose computer was an American computer called ENIAC, completed in 1946.

These early computers contained thousands of vacuum tubes and were massive machines that took up large rooms. With the development of first the *transistor* to replace vacuum tubes and then the *microchip*, which contains thousands of microscopic transistors linked together, computers became smaller and more and more powerful. A small home computer today is far more powerful than the first giant computers.

How a Computer Works A computer is a digital machine, which means that it does everything by numbers. It changes all the information it is given, including words, into code numbers called *binary code*. They actually consist of electric code signals that move along the wires in the computer and in and out of its microchips and other components.

These components handle the code signals in various ways. They can add two numbers together or compare two numbers to see if they are the same, for example, producing a result in the form of another code signal. They do these operations very quickly and the signals move at very high speed. Other components store the signals until they are needed. When the final result is produced, the computer changes it from a code signal into a form we can understand, such as words or numbers.

To operate, a computer has to follow a set of instructions that "tell" it how to perform a particular task. The set of instructions is called a *computer program*. The program is fed into the computer, where it is stored as a sequence of electric code signals. These code signals make the computer's components perform the correct sequence of operations to produce the result.

Computer Hardware The *hardware* of a computer system is the actual machinery—the computer itself and other equipment to which it is connected. The whole system has four basic parts, or units: the input, processor, memory, and output units. In microcomputers, which are small computers like those used at home, these units may all be linked together within one case. In minicomputers, mainframes, and supercomputers (large computers used in businesses) the units may be separate pieces that are connected together.

The *input* unit is used to feed information into the computer or to con-trol the computer as it operates. The keyboard is an important input unit; you use it to "type" in words and numbers and to press special keys that make things happen. Other input units include the mouse and joystick, which are hand-operated controls, and the light pen, which works by touching the screen of a computer. A voice recognition unit can respond to speech. You speak into it to give the computer information and commands.

The *memory* unit gives the computer the instructions that it needs. It also stores the information that comes from the input unit. There are several different kinds of memory units. The ROM (read-only memory) is a microchip inside the computer that contains *permanent* programs of instructions enabling the computer to work. The RAM (random-access memory) is another chip that stores programs and information for only as long as they are needed. New programs and information can be fed into RAM whenever required so that the computer can perform different tasks.

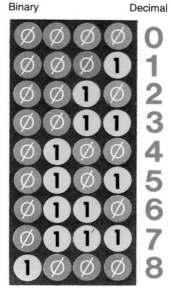

Binary   Decimal

▲ *A computer changes all the words and numbers fed into it into codes made up of 0s and 1s. The codes are known as* binary numbers.

▼ *This boy is playing with a computer "turtle" that draws geometrical shapes and patterns.*

▼ *A simple program for adding 2 and 2 together. It breaks the task into a series of small steps.*

10 LOAD NEXT BYTE INTO ACCUMULATOR
20 "2"
30 LOAD NEXT BYTE INTO REGISTER A
40 "2"
50 ADD NUMBER IN REGISTER A TO NUMBER IN ACCUMULATOR
60 STORE NUMBER IN ACCUMULATOR AT MEMORY LOCATION Y

▲ *This computerized security system allows one man to monitor a whole building. Various areas can be covered by the TV screens.*

Computer scientists today are working toward the ultra-intelligent machine—a machine that can think and learn from its own experience, just as we do. Many people think that sometime during the 21st century there will be computers that can work out problems and discover scientific laws better than humans can. In business, computers will run whole industries. At chess, they will beat all the Grand Masters. But it is doubtful whether a computer will ever write a play as well as Shakespeare did or compose a Mozart sonata.

These programs and information are stored outside the computer in a permanent form, such as a magnetic disk or tape. A memory unit such as a disk drive or tape player is used to feed the required program and information into the computer.

The *processor* unit is the brain of the computer. It follows the program instructions and takes the information from the memory or input units to produce a result. This result goes to the *output* unit, which is often a VDU (visual display unit) screen, like a television screen that displays words, numbers, and pictures. Other output units include a computer printer, a plotter that draws pictures, a speech synthesizer that talks, and a robot arm that moves. There is also a *modem*, which can send the output signals along telephone wires to a modem at the other end. This serves as an input unit for a computer at that end.

Computer Software The *software* of a computer consists of the various programs that make the computer do different things. The programs come on disks and tapes, and as chips that fit into the computer. Different kinds of software can turn the computer into a word processor, spreadsheet, or

database, which are common business uses for computers. There are also games and music software for entertainment, and educational software that makes the computer useful as a teaching aid.

Computer programmers write the programs that are sold as software. They work at the keyboard of a computer and feed in the various instructions. The computer itself works with code signals, which are not easily handled by the programmer. He or she, therefore, uses a "programming language" to write the program. The language often has English words to make it easy for the programmer to write and understand a program. Another program called a compiler, or interpreter, in the memory translates the language instructions into code signals.

ALSO READ: AUTOMATION; BABBAGE, CHARLES; BINARY CODE; CALCULATOR; ELECTRONICS.

GLOSSARY OF TERMS

Binary code The code of 0's and 1's that makes up computer "language."

Digital Using numbers; digital chips work with numerical quantities only.

Disk drive A memory unit used to feed a program or information into a computer from a magnetic disk.

Hardware Everything you can see and touch on a microcomputer.

Microchip Tiny piece of silicon that holds the electronic circuits in a computer.

Modem Equipment that turns computer signals into telephone signals and back again.

Program Software instructions that tell a computer how to solve a problem.

Software The programs that tell a computer what to do.

Transistor An electronic component that can be used as a switch or an amplifier; the principal component of microelectronic circuits.

VDU Visual display unit; a screen, as on a TV set, for displaying the output of a computer.